It Could Be Worse

The Social and Medical Adventures of a Young Doctor Traveling to Africa

Franklin V Cobos II, MD

iUniverse, Inc.
New York Bloomington

It Could Be Worse
The Social and Medical Adventures of a
Young Doctor Traveling to Africa

Copyright © 2009 by Franklin V Cobos II, MD

All rights reserved. No part of this book may be used or reproduced by any means, graphic, electronic, or mechanical, including photocopying, recording, taping or by any information storage retrieval system without the written permission of the publisher except in the case of brief quotations embodied in critical articles and reviews.

The views expressed in this work are solely those of the author and do not necessarily reflect the views of the publisher, and the publisher hereby disclaims any responsibility for them.

iUniverse books may be ordered through booksellers or by contacting:

iUniverse
1663 Liberty Drive
Bloomington, IN 47403
www.iuniverse.com
1-800-Authors (1-800-288-4677)

Because of the dynamic nature of the Internet, any Web addresses or links contained in this book may have changed since publication and may no longer be valid.

ISBN: 978-1-4401-7429-2 (sc)
ISBN: 978-1-4401-7431-5 (dj)
ISBN: 978-1-4401-7430-8 (ebk)

Printed in the United States of America

iUniverse rev. date: 11/05/2009

Contents

Introduction vii
From Paris with Love: The Asian Connection 1
Au Revoir 8
Getting There Is Half the Fun 12
Hospital Rounds 17
Rise 'n Shine 23
A Day at the River 27
A Day at the Market 31
Junk for Jesus 36
A Horse Is a Horse, of Course, of Course 42
Things That Go Bump in the Night 46
Step into the Sun 48
What's Cookin', Doc? 53
Back to Market 57
Malaria Strikes 60
Cat on a Hot Tin Roof 64
Things That Bleed in the Night 69
White Man Can't Jump 73
Just Another Day in Paradise 77
Two Is One, and One Is None 86
Peek and Shriek 89
Yes, I Am a Doctor, and This Is My Arabian Port-o-Potty 92
TWA: "Travel with Arabs" 98
Postscript 107
About the Author 108
Appendix: Advice for Newbies 109

Introduction

I drove home that evening after work just as I had nearly every other evening for years. I had worked about twelve hours that day in the University of Nebraska Medical Center where I'd spent my anesthesia residency, though at this point in time I was an assistant professor. It was a good job. I directed or performed anesthesia for nearly every type of surgery one could imagine, with the exception of lung transplants and pediatric cardiac cases. The wide variety of surgical challenges, teaching students and residents, along with doing some research of my own, kept the job stimulating and interesting. I liked nearly everyone with whom I worked. I was paid an enviable six-figure salary. And on this particular day I had received the results of my oral board exam, the most feared and dreaded test in an anesthesiologist's life. I had passed and was now officially a board-certified anesthesiologist. Yes, things were really going my way. If you asked, most people probably would say that as far as they could tell, I had finally arrived.

But arrived *where*? That was my question. And if I had truly arrived, then why wasn't I more excited or happy about it? Why did it seem so anticlimactic? Something still wasn't quite right. And what confused me as I drove home, almost on autopilot, was that while I seemed to be *doing* everything right with my life, I still did not *feel* right about it.

I slowly turned the car into the driveway, and stopped in front of the house. As I sat there in the new car I had purchased as my own graduation present, staring blankly through the windshield as the garage door opened automatically in front of me, I had an awkward revelation. It occurred to me that there was nothing left for me to do. The dramatic self-realization that I'd accomplished everything I had ever wanted since graduating from high school left me feeling surprisingly empty. I'd achieved the university acceptances, scholarships, awards, degrees, the research … all the accomplishments for which I had planned and worked so hard. But instead of the sense of fulfillment that one might well anticipate, there was an unexpected and surprisingly large void. Now what? What was I to do, now that I had done it all?

I pulled the car into the garage and stopped the engine. I sat there for a bit before slowly getting out, collecting my things from the trunk and then pushing the button on the wall to close the garage door. As I walked into the house, it seemed more still, more quiet than usual. Having been single my whole life, coming home to an empty house was not unusual. It was the norm. And after spending hours inside the maelstrom of frenzied panic that commonly characterizes the emergency room, intensive care units and operating rooms where I worked, the peace and quiet of my own home were comforting. You can only go on stamping out disease and dodging death and dying for so long before you need to come apart and rest a while. But now, in the moment, it seemed too peaceful, too quiet. In fact, for whatever reason, the quiet seemed deafening.

There was a time back in medical school when a married friend once told me that a childless house is a desolate place. I remember countering that while that may very well be true, it is also a neater and quieter place. I guess we were both right. I opened the fridge and looked inside for something of interest, partly because I didn't have anything else to do. *Nope. Not much in here. Maybe I should go grocery shopping.* I closed the door again. As it shut in front of me it was hard to ignore the fact, as I had for years, that mine was the only refrigerator door within my circle of friends that didn't have multiple pictures of family and friends plastered all over it. But I did have a magnet that had the number to call in case I smelled gas. And that said a lot. It said I needed to get out of the house, even if I didn't smell gas.

I walked down the hallway and turned into my office, where I wearily sat down in the chair behind my desk. I thought about turning on the computer, but for what? Why did I need to use it? I considered reading some of my anesthesia texts and studying a little, but for what? I had just spent the past twenty-four years studying and taking tests. I was done. I had passed. Suddenly I didn't have to do anything. What was it I wanted to do now? Who was I, and what did I really want? Had I fallen for the deception of defining myself by what I did at work and what I owned at home?

But what kind of a question was that? How could I possibly be unaware of my own identity? It seemed almost silly. Wasn't it obvious who I was? When people met and introductions were made, didn't they say, "This is Dr. Franklin Cobos?" That's my name, isn't it? Why is it that your name is wholly inadequate for describing your identity? Wasn't I the one who taught physiology and pharmacology to medical students, the one who trained nurses and doctors how to perform anesthesia? Wasn't I the one who conducted research, presented my findings at national meetings, and coauthored an article in a prominent, international journal within the specialty of anesthesia? Yes. Yes, I was. But had I chosen to merely *live to work* rather than *work to live* and, in doing so, reduced my identity to that of my job description?

All those facts, externally, were true. Yet, on the inside I felt uncertain. I felt like I was a cog on someone else's gear shaft, working toward their purposes, spending the larger portion of my life turning around and around, with a speed and in a direction chosen by somebody else. Perhaps it wasn't a question of uncertainty of who I was, but of who I wanted to become and, most important, who was going to be in charge of the change.

That night I went to bed with no real dreams of doing anything different the next day than I had that day, just a nagging sense that something had to change. And it had to change for the better. I turned off the lights and double-checked the alarm clock on the corner of the nightstand before rolling over in bed, closing my eyes with the discomforting knowledge that tomorrow would probably come and go just like any other day.

Two Years Later

"I can't believe you quit your job!" Suzanne said on the other end of the line, as my cousin and I spoke by telephone for the first time in years. She worked as an industrial engineer in San Francisco and had recently heard through the family grapevine that I was headed to Africa as a medical volunteer. She was fascinated about the idea. She had read stories on the Internet and in books about similar trips, and couldn't wait to talk with me. She was full of questions and disbelief that I actually had quit my job.

"I know, I know!," I told her. "But quitting was the only way I could work it out so that I can go for as long as I want. It was either quit and take control of every aspect of my life or just keep running on someone else's treadmill. So I got off the treadmill. It feels great!"

"Your friend James has some of the most amazing stories," she said. "I read the ones you sent to me and they are simply *unreal*." Dr. James Appel had graduated from Loma Linda University School of Medicine with me in the same class. After completing residency, he had gone to Africa semi-permanently to run a rural hospital, though he stayed in touch with family and friends through the Internet by sending interesting stories and pictures.

"And all true," I replied. "I remember he and I used talk over lunch and dream about doing medicine in Africa after we finished with residency. We thought that would be so cool!"

"Now, exactly how long has he been over there?"

"Five years. He went to Chad right after finishing his residency and has been there ever since. It's a tough job, one doctor trying to run an entire hospital. It can be especially challenging since he doesn't have any trained anesthesia providers to help him do his surgeries. That's part of why I offered to go."

"I can't imagine how incredible a trip like that would be," said Suzanne. "I would *love* to do something like that one day. I'd do it in a heartbeat!"

"Well, I'm getting ready to go. You wanna come?"

"Do I? Yes!" she exclaimed excitedly. I could almost hear her jumping up and down on the other end of the line.

"Now, just hold you horses." I needed her to calm her down. "Excluding the possibility of *you* quitting *your* job, how much time do you think you can take off?"

"Oh, I've got tons of vacation time built up," she said. "I've worked here for ages with no time off, ever. I never take vacation. This job is really getting old. I just need to get out! Besides, I've wanted to do this kind of thing for years."

"Well, going to Chad would definitely be 'getting out.' Compared to the U.S., it's a very different place to be in. It's hot, mostly desert, they don't speak English, and they're predominantly Muslim."

"Okay. Well … how long are you going to go for? Wait! How much will it cost me?" I told her. The line went quiet. "Suzanne?" I waited. Nothing. "Suzanne? You there?" I heard coughing in the background, then her wheezing voice as she sputtered, "How much did you just say?!" I repeated myself. "Are you serious?! Sorry about that cuz… I aspirated and choked on my Muslix before some of it blew out my nose."

And so the discussion and planning started in earnest, and for the next few months it was all I could do to keep Suzanne from quitting her job and going without me. There were plenty of things to keep us busy in the meantime, though. She had to get a passport and purchase an entry visa from the Chadian embassy in Washington, D.C., which was sent to her only three days before we left. There were multiple doctor's appointments and five vaccinations she didn't want but had to get. We went shopped online together for mosquito nets and other travel essentials. And since French was the official language in Chad and because we had to fly through Paris to get to N'Djamena, the Chadian capital city, we studied French in our spare time. After all, we could spend four days in Paris before continuing to Africa. What better place was there to practice speaking French?

The days quickly passed into weeks and a few months later, in October 2008, I called her from the airport in Omaha. "Good morning. Hey, you wanna come to Africa with me today?" She laughed and said, "You're on! But I'll see you in Paris first."

From Paris with Love: The Asian Connection

Arriving from different points of origin, Suzanne and I had to rendezvous at the hostel where we'd stay in Paris; then we saw some sights in the afternoon. During our early planning, our mutual decision had been to stay in a hostel rather than a more swank location. The reasons were simple. First of all, we wanted to mingle with all the younger travel and adventure types who frequent hostels, meeting people with whom we could practice both French and English. In addition, we thought that, compared to Africa, anything in Paris would feel like a five-star hotel. Finally, the money we saved likely would be enough to feed and clothe both of us during our entire stay in Chad.

During our last conversation in the States, we confirmed directions to the hostel and made an emergency plan to meet up in case we couldn't find the place and were without means of communication. Fortunately for us, we didn't need to execute this plan. It did, however, take me about three hours to reach the hostel, and it took Suzanne four. This was due to a combination of factors. The top two were the fact that neither of us had slept very much in the past twenty-four hours, and neither of us was very enthusiastic about dragging a hundred pounds of luggage each through the Paris Metro, up and down stairs via underground walkways between train lines. I spent my time waiting for Suzanne by wandering the streets surrounding our hostel, trying to not look too American or too sleep-deprived. I feared the locals would mistake me for a street bum, staggering down the street past all the baked goodies in every other store window, drooling as I paused to stare, hoping my travel partner would arrive soon so we could celebrate with a huge lunch and then hit the town.

Finally we settled into the hostel after a prolonged and confused discussion with a non-French, "Frenglish"-speaking host, whose malodorous fragrance filled the whole room, justifying the argument that the French originate the finest perfumes on earth largely out of necessity. He refused to let us into our room, but did direct us downstairs, which mercifully was also downwind, where we could store our luggage until the official check-in opened at four p.m. I nearly fell down the stairs with my three bags trailing behind me as we descended into what seemed to be an old Roman dungeon. After carefully steadying my feet on the damp stone tile steps, I turned left and promptly had another close call when my forehead nearly struck the low ceiling archway that lead around and down into the crypt below. I hesitantly crept forward as I worked my way through the catacombs, certain that I would see an iron maiden or rack in the room where we were to leave the luggage. But all that was there was a sump pump.

We ascended from the dungeon and made our escape to find lunch. After feasting on what seemed like the best food we'd eaten in days, we returned at the appointed time to claim our reservation. We were assigned a room on the ground floor (not to be confused with the first floor as it is called in America). This so-called room would be more accurately described as a concrete box, and it was already occupied by two Asian girls staying in the "loft," i.e., a cement cage joined to our room via a small spiral staircase in the corner. In the other cramped corner was a small closet containing a shower and tiny toilet, with part of the seat cut off so it could be put down and not get stuck on the wall, which was flush with the side of the bowl. An initial inspection revealed that the Asians had not mastered how to keep all the water behind the shower curtain and prevent it from flooding the three and a half tiles of floor space in the "bathroom" and flowing under the doorway and out into our room. Well, we thought, it could be worse. At least we had a shower and toilet. Upstairs, all they had was a sink.

We went to the Louvre as our first stop and enjoyed an audio tour of ancient Greece, Rome, and Mesopotamia. As the tracks played on my iPod through a stereo doubler, our path took us past the *Mona Lisa* and some of the most important works of art in Western history. This day trip into the past was complicated, unfortunately, by the fact that many times European museums (especially the big ones) will relocate pieces, remodel rooms, and redirect the flow of guests without warning. As a result, you may not be able to find something that is indicated clearly on the map as being right in front of you and that, in most cases, you flew from the other side of the earth to see. Once we were looking for an important piece from ancient Greece. We actually swallowed our tourist pride and asked for directions from a French museum worker standing around doing nothing nearby. I hesitated at first, as he seemed to be intently waiting for a reason to go on strike ... and do more nothing. He and his prim and proper colleague claimed that what we were seeking was on permanent display in London. "Au contraire, mon frère!" I thought. "I've been there, and I've been here, and I can assure you, it is definitely *here*." I thanked them politely, in French, and bid them adieu, leaving them alone with their snide snickers directed in our general direction. Sooner rather than later, we found it by accident, despite the misguided directions from the French museum staffers.

The architecture of the Louvre itself is something to see. The museum used to be the home of the French kings, though for one of them who grew up there, Louis XIV, it was a bit too much to live in the city all the time. So, he built Versailles out in the country, about ten miles away from Paris, to get away from city life.

When we returned to the hostel, we discovered a whole flock of Asians had descended en mass and were inhabiting the dining/socializing area. There also was one English-speaking guy, who showed us how to tap into the wireless network from the bar across the street so we could send email for free. There was an expensive email kiosk there in our hostel lobby, but why pay for something you can get for free, mon ami? Though we were limited to twenty minutes, it turned out to be an effective mode of communication. Which was all we really wanted, other than a *really* good night's sleep. In the room, not surprisingly, the floor was flooded again. "Dang Asians!" we thought. But it turned out that while we were absent during the day, the two Asian girls previously staying in the loft had been swapped out for a new pair of Aryan giants. (Seriously, the cute one was really tall! I'm talking Viking warrior princess, super-size-me tall. Not that I stared or anything.) Well, at least I could talk with these women. All it took was one or two of the three or four complete sentences I could still remember from a year of German in college, and they both opened up a bit in English.

We quickly discovered the main drawback of our room was that everyone on the first floor had to come by us on the way to their own rooms. Our door was just across the hall from the eating/socializing area. And why, pray tell, should that matter? Well, if you're from Asia and visiting Paris, and it's one o'clock in the morning, it's actually seven a.m. where your brain lives (and lives quite loudly, evidently). So, why wouldn't you chatter away, making sounds like silverware falling down stone stairs to the luggage hold so that everyone within two metro stops around can enjoy the sounds of your frivolity? I mean, it makes perfect sense … if you don't actually think about it. I always travel with earplugs and eyeshades so I was prepared. And fortunately, Suzanne had kept those very supplies from the Air France flight that had brought her to Paris from San Francisco. So we both were able largely to block out the very rude world around us and dream of ways we could return the favor to these people when we got up the next morning.

The next morning we went out to eat and found very simple fare—a baguette *sans/avec* butter and/or jam, hot milk/chocolate. Period. "Dude!" I thought, "How could I have forgotten all about the dearth of breakfast food on the "continent" (hence the term "continental breakfast.") We finished and promptly left to find a shop that would be open early and would sell us something reminiscent of what I would call breakfast, totally forgetting our vow to rain down revenge on all those Asian chatterboxes.

After we filled our bellies with some finer French cuisine, we chose to spend the entire day exploring Versailles. It took forty minutes to get there by train and ten minutes to purchase a Paris museum pass from a snooty tourist office worker. With the pass, we were whisked into Versailles VIP style without having to wait with the hoi-polloi whose ancestors, centuries before, supposedly were told "Let them eat cake." This is where we failed to learn yet another lesson about not asking for directions. It occurred at the end of our very long day there. We were tired, we hadn't gotten the high-quality sleep we had hoped to have, thanks to our new German roommates. We were really tired of walking; at least we weren't carrying a hundred pounds of luggage each. So we broke down and, against our better judgment, asked in French for directions. All we wanted to know was where the *sortie* (exit) was. The French gardener politely sent us to the other side of the garden, where he was certain an exit would let us out on the road we were to follow back to the king's chambers. Ten minutes later, with no cheese at the end of the maze, we found a locked gate in the general direction the gardener had sent us. We wandered another fifteen minutes before we got out of that area, which was hedged with bushes, and headed away from the queen's mansion, up the road to the main entrance, and finally out of Versailles. From there it was back to the train station, and then we enjoyed a thirty-minute nap on the way back to Paris. There, we ate crepes at a delightful cafe on rue Cler, got our second wind, and then visited the Arc de Triomphe. We climbed to the top and saw the impressive Eiffel Tower light show that takes place at the top of every hour. It lasted ten minutes, lighting up the whole tower in a blue glow accented with white sparkles and the distinctive circle of gold stars that symbolizes the European Union.

The next morning we embarked on a tour of the Musée d'Orsay via the Place de la Concorde, where they once chopped people's heads off in the public square, and the Champs de Élyssées, where the Tour de France bike race ends, usually with American Lance Armstrong in the lead. We broke for lunch to do some people watching and enjoy some more fine cuisine. While waiting, it was hard not to notice how beautiful the French women are (Suzanne agrees). It's interesting though, the really hot ones have really ugly little dogs. I personally believe it something the women do on purpose in a vain attempt to accentuate their own beauty. In any case, all I can say is "*Vive la France*! *Vive la différence!* One lady, who must have been about fifty-five years old, pedaled by during her lunch break wearing gold stilettos, gold-colored fishnet panty hose, and a matching, short, gold leather jacket.

After we recovered from that sight, and finishing the most exquisite French Vanilla ice cream I have ever tasted, we went to see the *Thinker* and *The Kiss*, sculptures by Rodin. Then we went to Napoleon's tomb and the museums dedicated to World War I and World War II. Afterward, we found another fantastic cafe on rue Cler; I'm not sure there were any that weren't. Dinner was great, and the snooty lady whose big black dog blocked the waitress's pathway created quite the scene, providing more than adequate entertainment for the evening. The one word I recognized was one the waitress used after this woman left: "Hallelujah!" My sentiments exactly. And with that, we went back to noisy land for an attempt at some sleep.

Prior to going to bed, I tried to check email on my Mac out in the eating area. As I struggled to hack into the system across the street, a sexy accent asked me if I spoke French. At the moment I looked up to see who it was, I cannot tell you how much I wanted to say "oui." You see, the young woman, who spoke English in an even sexier accent, turned out to have competed in the Miss Switzerland pageant; she had been working and traveling on a cruise ship for the past five months. She wanted to charge up her Mac but didn't have the correct plug adapter for France. I assured her that I had what she needed and retrieved my own cord and power adapter from my room. We spent the next two hours traveling the world together through photos we'd each taken over the past year, exchanged email addresses, and decided to meet for breakfast.

Just before I turned in, I was approached by the curry-infused Indian desk clerk, who asked if, as a favor, I would trade beds with a little Chinese girl who had arrived at 10:30 p.m. without a reservation so that she wouldn't have to share a room with two guys upstairs in the only vacant bed available. I reluctantly agreed, but only for one night. When I went upstairs and knocked on the door, however, the guys wouldn't answer or let me in. I came back down and tried to talk to desk clerk but could not for the life of me convince him that I was unable to get into the room. (There is only one key for each room; don't ask me why.) Finally, he gave me his master electronic key; I took it and stomped upstairs. After deftly swiping it and whooshing the door open I was met by a Spaniard, gape-mouthed, clearly confused as to why his room was being invaded by this stranger. Irritated, I looked straight at him and asked, "Why didn't you just open the door?" He answered with a non sequitur, as I pushed my way in past him to set up camp for the night.

Shortly thereafter, a Chinese man came in, reeking of rotten Mandarin … or socks. I couldn't quite tell which; frankly at that hour of the night, I could not have cared less and as a doctor, I've smelled far worse. I settled in on the bottom bunk, the Chinese man was up top, and the snoring Spanish fellow was off on the other side of the room. For the next four hours I could hear and feel my bunkmate shift and toss and turn, and he robbed me of my sleep. Unknown to me, one floor down, Suzanne was having the very same experience with the Chinese girl. In retrospect, it is clear that those birds of a feather really should have been put in a flock together.

The next morning Suzanne took one for the team and fended for herself while I met one on one with Swiss miss for hot chocolate and pleasant conversation over breakfast. Ah, the joys of having a beautiful and intelligent, well traveled woman for company. It doesn't get any better than this, I thought to myself. But alas all good things do come to an end, including breakfast. So we said our final farewells and parted company.

Suzanne and I took in the sights; we saw Sainte Chapelle, Notre Dame and the crypt below it, the Pantheon, Trocadero, and Eiffel Tower. On the way to the last stop, where we purchased some more vanilla ice cream to fuel our final evening's activities in Paris, we spotted an elderly, balding man with Coke-bottle glasses, seated crossed-leg, smoking like a petite chimney, wearing a blue pin-striped suit, brown shoes and screaming bleach-white socks. The fashion faux pas was shocking, even to an American like me. His arrogance seemed to suggest, "I am so French, I can get away with this and still look good!" *Au contraire, mon frère.* Further ahead, we spotted some Arabs dressed in black suits and brown leather shoes. It was like we were looking at a pack of Doberman Pinschers. I was waiting for the voice of Higgins from *Magnum, P.I.* to call out, "Lads! Chase!" After taking a seat on a bench under the shadow of the Eiffel Tower, we decided to continue amusing ourselves by acting as unofficial fashion police. Seated side by side, cross-legged, Suzanne and I licked our dripping ice cream in sync while deeply frowning at each other as one woman passed in front of us, parading around in long stockings the color of which could easily have been described as Yak's Yak Yellow. Enjoying our new self-appointed role of Paris fashion police, we began mentally issuing tickets for the more gross violations of fashion sense. We caught one lady waiting in line to climb the tower who was wearing rhinestone-studded jeans with triangles opening up the sides of both legs, followed closely by another lady wearing black stockings with the same style effects. By all appearances, the older lady was the mother of the younger, who also had a toddler following her. Shortly thereafter an old lady, who appeared to be dressed as a gypsy, entered the scene and seemed to be trying to talk to the younger of the two fashion victims. While trying to decide what collective fine to impose on this group, it suddenly dawned on us that this was no ordinary gypsy working the crowd, but rather great gram-grams, the top family figure for the other three succeeding generations. It was a lot like seeing a real live Russian babushka doll taken apart!

Au Revoir

The next day we physically and mentally regrouped by sleeping in and doing little else besides checking email and making the trip to the airport. We emailed a lot of news to a lot of people because we really weren't sure if or when we'd be able to contact the outside world again. We knew James could send email from Chad, but we had no idea whether or not the capability to do so would continue during our stay. We decided to arrive at the airport early, suspecting that the more time we had to spare, the easier it would be to deal with any unforeseen delays that might make us miss the only flight into Chad for the next few days.

We arrived at Charles de Gaulle International Airport about an hour and a half before we would board the plane. We entered the large ticketing and check-in area and stopped in front of the great big display board to see the counter for our airline and the gate for our flight. Well, after searching the display board, we could see that our flight's check-in area was in zone nine. But we were standing in zone two, so we did a right face and started rolling toward zone nine, luggage in tow. Immediately, two policemen and three French machine gunners stopped us and pressed us and the crowd back about five feet, blocking our way to zone nine. After a few moments a policewoman told us in English that a suitcase had been left unattended fifty feet away (we could look over and see it). Officials suspected it was a bomb, and they were securing the terminal. All flights were being either put on hold or cancelled. "Well, you do what you gotta do I suppose," I thought, "but how am I going to get to Chad?"

As we waited helplessly within the secured zone, looking at this blue tote bag all by itself in the middle of the departure terminal walk way, we decided to beg the guy at the ticket counter in zone two to check us onto our flight. We walked right back over to his desk, unhindered by the line that had been dispersed by the police. Unfortunately for us, the snooty little man refused although he then said that if we were still blocked from zone nine in thirty minutes, when they would close the check-in for our flight, he would take care of us. But once we made this Franco-American pact, we were herded out of the terminal by the police as the loudspeaker informed us that all flights were now officially cancelled. Sweet. We had been so close, so very, very close. Goodbye, Chad trip!

For the next thirty minutes, we stood on the sidewalk outside the terminal with all the other passengers; police cars with their sirens blaring whizzed around the place. We met and mingled with people from all over the world, awkwardly chatting while we stood a stone's throw from an explosion waiting to happen. Meanwhile, the bomb squad went in to take care of business.

And care for it they did. They put the thing in a box, right there where they found it and blew it straight to heaven. The explosion was quite loud, though the ground didn't noticeably shake beneath our feet. Surprisingly, within five minutes, it was business as usual. We were led straight back into the terminal, past a lady sweeping up some charred paper off the floor. We casually strode along the walkway as people sipped wine in a café off to the side. Everyone seemed to take the potential bomb in stride.

We grabbed the last copy of an English newspaper we would see for ages and hurriedly walked onto the plane, the last two people to board, with only three minutes to spare. James and his wife Sarah had asked us to get the paper, to give them a glimpse at the outside world. The boldfaced headline read "World Markets Crashing" with figures and images showing 20- to 24-percent losses that day in London, Tokyo, New York, and Germany. From all indicators, it looked like it would be a good time to drop off the face of the earth for a while. I folded the newspaper in half, tucked it under my arm, boarded the plan and hoped my investment advisor knew what he was doing.

In my opinion, our flight to N'Djamena was uneventful. Suzanne might have disagreed, though, because she had to sit next to a chain smoker whose seven cigarettes per hour routine came to a screeching halt for the duration of the trip. Instead, he created endless, anxious chatter as he attempted to drown his nicotine urge with wine. After losing track of how many bottles he had soused himself with and watching him spill some of his stinky, red swill on his trousers, she eventually was able to ignore him. I, however, enjoyed the luxurious silence afforded by my set of earplugs and eyeshades. Suzanne was too polite to use hers.

Our flight of fancy finally ended as we touched down at the airport in N'Djamena. The door opened, and we descended a set of stairs that were rolled up to the side of the plane, not unlike the President and First lady when they leave Air Force One. Here, though, there was no marching band or red carpet to meet us. There was, however, a bus that looked relatively new at the bottom of the stairs, which would drive us thirty yards across the tarmac to the terminal. I have no idea why we were driven that far. Maybe they thought the poor white foreigners would be exhausted if they had to move their flaccid, pampered bodies over that long of a distance. More likely though, the reason was the possibility of us getting lost on the way. Seriously. See, it was absolutely pitch dark there. You could stumble around in the darkness all night long if you headed off in the wrong direction. I was told that only five years ago there had been no lights in the entire city. It seemed clear why Africa had been called the Dark Continent.

We left the bus and climbed the short set of steps that led us to the customs and immigration officials inside the airport building, where we were glad to find working lights. One drawback of this modern convenience was that it attracted enough insects to fill a feature-length program of *Mutual of Omaha's Wild Kingdom*. Bugs were absolutely everywhere. Not a good sign, boys and girls, particularly since Suzanne hates bugs. They flew around us in the night air, landing in our hair and on our clothes. They were on my back, they were on other people's backs. They were crawling all over the ground, some dead and crunching under our footsteps. If we were in Asia, I would have said it sounded like we were stepping on fortune cookies. But this was Africa. So I used my passport as a fan/fly swatter as we stood dead last in line. Well, more accurately, just last in line.

Finally it was our turn, and we stepped forward to hand our papers to the immigration officer. He didn't speak any English. Not even Frenglish, or Engrish, for that matter. No surprise there. Now, for the past month, I had been studying a bit of French in my spare time and so I tried to explain who we were and why we had come. He looked at us with an expression that seemed to say I wasn't going to get a passing grade on this oral exam. Lucky for me, James had written a letter of invitation in French, which I had handed to him with our passports and that seemed to satisfy his questions more than my linguistic foibles did. I don't recall if he rolled his eyes at us as he stamped our passports and handed them back as another officer pantomimed that we needed to register with the police within three days. (Yes, I can count all of the fingers you are holding up, officer, thank you). OK, fine. We promised to turn ourselves into the police within three days so we could be questioned and bribed beyond all recognition. Thanks. At this point in time, it was so late at night and the language barrier was so high that I think they just waved us through because they were tired. We were the last people on the last flight in and were the last obstacle they needed to negotiate before getting off work and going home. This turned out to be exceptionally fortuitous for me because I had forgotten my yellow fever vaccination documentation. Had they remembered to ask for it, they could've denied me entry into the country. Sometimes it's better to be lucky than to be good.

From there we went to see if our luggage had arrived in the same city and country, if not the same continent, that we had. As we passed through the door way, we were immediately met by a man calling us by name. Initially, this might seem a bit unnerving, but when you consider that we were the only white people on the plane, they were expecting us, and that we were the last ones through the door … it was kind of a no-brainer. Accompanied by the hospital representative who had come to meet us, we stopped to collect our luggage, which appeared to be guarded by a group of porters. They were mysteriously eager to get our bags for us and load them onto the one and only wheeled baggage cart, only two of whose wheels actually turned. We offered to open up all our bags for customs, but it seemed as though they were about as tired and as eager to get rid of us as the immigration officers had been, and they, too, just waved us on through.

When we got to the taxi in front of the building, the lead porter demanded that I pay him fifty euros in exchange for his services. He vociferously protested when I told him there was no way I would give him more than five. "Fine, you don't want five euros?" I asked him. "That's your choice. I won't force them on you. What about getting no euros? How's that sound right about now?" I turned my back on him, perhaps not the smartest thing to do in Africa, as I turned to get into the car with Suzanne. I swear it's like they looked at me and all they saw was a white, walking piggy bank. After a brief and angry exchange with the porters, we slammed the doors of the taxi and went careening off into the hot, unlit Chadian night.

Getting There Is Half the Fun

We spent the night in N'Djamena at a language institute, where we got acclimated to the culture, climate, and living conditions. Although I had been to Kenya for a month during my fourth year of medical school, my cousin Suzanne had not been in a third-world nation before. And for her, the first encounter with Africa was something she will never forget. All five of the human senses seem as though they are on overload as the mind tries to process all the newness of everything, some of it delightful new and interesting, some of it revolting or even frightening. It was the sights and smells of the streets that quickly captivated Suzanne's attention. The smell of garbage and animal waste wafted into our faces as the hot breeze swirled around us. This made walking alongside the dirt roads that ran throughout the city and toward the main market an oppressive journey. The poverty-stricken examples of humanity that dotted the city left pock marks on all but the hardest of hearts who see them. At first, you want to help them all, but eventually one must be content helping only some. The obvious question you struggle with first is, "*How* do people live like this?!" This is quickly followed by, "*Why* do people live like this?" The answers to both are complex, and for me, have never been clear or easily elucidated.

From N'Djamena, we would travel south six hours by automobile (hopefully) over (mostly) paved road to Kelo. There, we would meet James, my Y2K classmate from Loma Linda University. James came directly to Chad after completing his residency in Ventura California and had been there at that point for the better part of five years. He and I had lost touch for a long time after graduation, but after a few email exchanges I was eager to join him for a while in Africa and see how I could help out. Through these emails I learned that during his stay he had not had any trained anesthesia personnel to help him manage his frequent surgical cases. Limited supplies dictated that I would essentially have to practice anesthesia as it existed before the advent of inhaled anesthetics (and maybe even electricity). Other than spinal anesthesia, the only anesthetic available was intravenous ketamine. He had no oxygen tanks, no inhaled anesthetics, and no functional anesthesia machine. It was exactly the challenge for which I'd been looking. After all, it couldn't get much worse than this. How could I not be helpful?

Before leaving for Kelo, we stopped at the market in downtown N'Djamena to pick up a few essentials that Sarah, James's Danish wife, requested that we purchase. One of the most important acquisitions was good, old-fashioned toilet paper, a modern convenience that apparently has yet to catch on in this part of the world. (Yes, you do have to be wary of people's left hands.) We were told that the capital was the only city in the nation where one could actually buy any toilet paper, and I jokingly wondered if that's why they built the airport there. A very limited supply of vegetables, jam, and Tabasco-like sauce rounded out the luxuries we were to hunt down during our brief detour. Batteries were exceptionally hard to come by. The AAA size does not exist, and AAs cost nearly $4 a piece. Most of the market is comprised of people selling cloth, clothing, sandals, and sunglasses. If I had my way, I'd open up a men's and women's fragrance section. There was also a wide selection of what I presumed were pirated movies crammed onto $3 DVDs with four to sixteen full-length feature films on each one. I have no idea how they do it, but I suppose if they can put fifty people in a minibus, fitting a dozen or so movies onto a single DVD isn't such a miracle.

It is worth mentioning that Suzanne created quite a stir among the other market goers. Suzanne is your typical young woman from the United States, and she chose to wear what any other girl from San Francisco might wear on a sweltering hot day while shopping at the outdoor market—a sleeveless cotton dress that came to just above her knees. And to top it all off, she had nothing covering her head or hair. I lost track of how many men stopped me to reprimand me for not having my woman's head covered or for letting her walk around "naked" with bare shoulders. In their eyes, the sight of this petite feminine form parading about the market in such a manner was practically pornographic. These repeated, heartfelt conversations usually ended with them also trying to convince me to vote for Obama in the upcoming elections or to purchase a Nylon trifold wallet with a Velcro closure featuring a Chadian flag, American flag, and the face of Osama Bin Laden on its three sections. I suppose I could have used it to carry my passport, but presenting it to customs back in Atlanta could generate unnecessary questions, so I always declined before heading off into the next stall to see where "my woman" had gone off to without me. Suzanne just rolled her eyes, continued her shopping, and said, "Women of Chad, liberate yourselves!"

After concluding our shopping adventure, we loaded up all our stash for the ride to Kelo. We also picked up two Canadians and one Dane before leaving N'Djamena for Bere. This leg of the journey took us over mostly paved road, making the half day drive more tolerable than we'd expected. James had warned us via email that since the rainy season was ending, the road beyond Kelo would be difficult to pass and much of it still would likely be flooded. There was even a small chance we would not be met by anyone from Bere, since they might be flooded in to their location and unable to reach us. But that was the worst-case scenario. Next to worse, and more likely, was that we would have to rent a small fleet of motorcycles to take ourselves and our luggage on the axle-deep drive through the areas in which cars and trucks would be stuck so deep in the mud we would be forced to abandon them.

Without telling Suzanne about these very real possibilities, I sat quietly with my own thoughts as we pulled into Kelo, all the while eagerly watching for a tall white guy with whom I used to go to medical school. Although I did not have explicit instructions for how we would meet up, I actually didn't expect our meeting to be that much of a challenge. I figured it would be a lot like an easy version of *Where's Waldo*.

Our minivan pulled up in front of a ragged collection of (and, I use the term loosely) buildings, and we all spilled out the side doors to stretch our legs and search for a source of clean drinking water. I walked to the back of the van and turned to look up and down the street. There was a large gathering of Chadians gathered around a dark blue 4X4 Toyota truck and a nearly shaven, white skinned head rising out of the crowd. Ah, yes, that would be James.

Wow. Long time no see! I remembered him having more hair and more meat on his now skinny six-foot-plus frame.

He turned to greet me with a grin, "Franklin, welcome to Kelo." We shook hands as he was very quickly pulled back into the verbal fray of the French jousting that was required before he could negotiate a rate for us to hire the only vehicle capable of making it from Kelo to Bere over the muddy path referred to as "the road." He warned me to herd up the rest of the light skins and stay out of sight. If the locals got too much of an idea that this rental was for a pack of rich white people, they would levy a heavy "need it" tax on us (not to be confused with the unrelated "want it" tax applied frequently to items in the United States and Europe). I quickly walked away to warn the others of our pending fiscal peril.

We half-way hid out behind the minivan and took in the sights and sounds of this frontier shanty town. Kelo is a collection of shacks, really, not so much a town that a Westerner might envision. One section of one shack is a functioning post office, receiving precious parcel-post packages from the United States to the tune of $18 per small package. There is no gas station. Just a guy who sells small quantities in glass beverage bottles, set out on a wooden table for display (That's how you know there's gas!). There's no bank, but we had already met money changes in the main market in N'Djamena, so getting money wasn't a problem. Getting robbed, that might be a problem, though.

James negotiated a price we could afford. Afterward, we somehow managed to pile all our luggage in the back of the truck bed, cram a total of seven people in the truck's cab, and five people on top of the luggage. They clung on for dear life as the truck jostled over the "road" toward Bere, while the rest of us inside the cab, at times, did a fine impression of pop corn in a hot air popper. Truly, it was African-style transportation at its finest.

One advantage the rutted roads do afford the weary traveler is a slow panorama of absolute wilderness and pristine beauty. This usually occurs as the truck slows to enter, traverse, and then emerge from pot holes the size of kiddy pools. It's wild country, just like I remembered seeing in *National Geographic* magazine when I was in grade school. It's raw nature, with the sky as your limit.

Eventually, as night was just starting to fall, we came to a river crossing. This was the last obstacle (that we knew of) before we arrived at the hospital in Bere. There was a bridge being built nearby, but for now, we would have to be taken across by barge—actually, a pair of large pontoon-like floaters with various scraps of planks and tree branches forming a platform onto which one might even dare to drive his vehicle. If he were really desperate. Like I was. At that moment. After the truck was onboard, we began our trip across the river, about a hundred feet. This was accomplished manually by a couple of strapping young African men pulling on a rope that was tied to the far shore. Like most technology on the continent, this mechanism was slow, needed no electricity, had no moving parts, required no advanced training and education to operate, and broke down only underneath a lack of human will. Or, how shall I say… insufficient funds? But it was a nice start to a storybook adventure.

Now, don't get me wrong. For several reasons, this wasn't the Jungle Adventure ride at Disneyworld. For one, the snakes, hippos, and crocks in Chad are real. And unfortunately, sometimes you do have to get out and push your own ride. This happened well after dark had descended around us, about thirty minutes after we left the barge behind us for the last leg of the journey. The driver made a rookie error in wilderness driving, and before James could prevent him from doing so, he landed the front left tire nearly axle deep in mud as he swerved to try to miss one of the numerous ruts the rain had left in the road. While this was all very irritating, it didn't surprise me one bit.

I got out of the car and sized up the problem with the other men, who also had the foresight to bring flashlights. The mud was wet, slick, and had clogged most of the tire treads . We needed dry dirt that would give the wheel more traction as it drove out of the rut. Dirt we had. Dry dirt, though, even though we were near the Sahara, was a problem. I started looking around for some other ideas (cue music from *MacGyver* here). As I walked in front of the truck, I noticed a short palm tree nearby. The dead fronds near the base were hardened, dry, and coarse. Just what the doctor ordered. I whipped out my Swiss Army knife and proceeded to cut off as many as I thought could be stuffed under the car tire before we half pushed, half drove the car out of the soft mud. And though I do admit that the twelve men who wandered out of the night and onto the scene and helped us push the truck from behind had something to do with our successful extrication, I remain unconvinced they were angels. This is largely because they demanded payment for services rendered and were pretty angry when we refused to give them any.

A little while later, fourteen hours after packing up our things that morning in N'Djamena, we finally reached Bere. We were greeted by friendly smiles and faces lit up by LED flashlights as we were led into the guest house and shown to our rooms. Exhausted, we eagerly washed our dusty faces and brushed the fuzzy feeling off our teeth. Then we hung our mosquito nets, and lay down on our wooden bunk beds, quickly falling asleep on the thin foam mattresses. The morning would come too soon.

Hospital Rounds

Given the limited supplies of electricity, life at the hospital in Bere is naturally and easily scheduled around the rising and setting of the sun, which at a latitude of 11 degrees south, occurs at nearly the same time every day, all year long. Daybreak and sunset occur around five a.m. and six p.m., respectively. We get up because the sun wakes us up; we go to sleep because it's dark. Besides, even if you did stay up late, there's no TV to watch, and the one book you brought to read on the plane ... well, you already read that one.

After getting up and having "breakfast" (nothing more than slices of bread), Suzanne and I joined James and the other hospital staff for rounds. The hospital has a capacity for about seventy patients, which can make for some very long days, especially if you're the only doctor there. I remember when I was an intern and I would feel that taking care of more than five or six inpatients was challenging. Hah! Those were the days.

As we made our way through the first part of the morning, James explained how recent local events had affected the hospital patient population and workload. Things had gotten relatively quiet, and work was slower than usual (meaning there were only about forty patients instead of the full capacity of seventy). This was because of fear. People were afraid of coming to the hospital and getting killed. There was an altercation between some local African and Arab clansmen when an Arab cow wandered into an African's rice field and did some damage. While in the West we might say, "like a bull in a china shop," here it's "like a cow in a rice field." Well, the next thing you know the owner of the field and the owner of the cow had taken matters of justice into their own hands. One of them was so badly beaten and wounded that he was taken for dead. As a result, a small culture war erupted, leaving five dead and fourteen wounded; most of these were women and children, and all of them came to the hospital for care. Here's the kicker though: later that day the guy who was thought to be dead revived. I couldn't help but feel an acute urge to translate into Arabic the quote by Mark Twain, "The reports of my death were greatly exaggerated." I can see it now, silk-screened onto a T-shirt, along with a caricature of a turban-wearing Twain on camel back. I bet you it would be a big hit in the Islamic world. In any event, people were afraid to come to the hospital because they thought they accidentally might get caught up in the fray. For that reason, the outpatient service had ground to a halt, and as patient discharges were not accompanied by new admittances, the hospital staff had a lighter load to carry.

To the western mind, the idea of a world without law and order is a concept of the past, a condition that existed in a time long ago, someplace far away. Truth be told, much of the world still runs with neither law nor order. Or, at least without what I would call law and order. In Chad, I saw no police officers once we left N'Djamena. There were no courts of law. Guns were possessed only by the police or soldiers, so the rest of the population is left to fend for itself with primitive weapons, skill, and cunning. Chad has more of a Darwinian type of society, where survival depends on strength, raw intellect, and acquisition and use of natural resources. If you think about it, Chad is very much like the free market of the West. It's just Chadians don't really have any rules that are enforced by governing bodies. But I repeat myself.

Rounds in the hospital are done in French, one of two official languages in Chad; the other is Chadian Arabic. Suzanne and I had tried to study French on our own back in the States and in Paris in an effort to ease the transition. James still had to translate a lot for us just so we could tell what was happening. Given all the patients we saw, all the different problems each one of them had, and all the talking in unfamiliar local dialects being translated into French or

Arabic and then into English, it all quickly became a confusing blur for me. But I will tell you a few of the more memorable cases from the first day.

Some of the first images that come to mind when one thinks of Africa are those of frail, starving, skinny framed figures reminiscent of prisoners who were kept in Auschwitz or some other World War II concentration camp. There certainly are those types of patients in Bere. The stories behind the lean figures are not as uniform as those from wartime Germany. One was a patient with AIDS who had been misdiagnosed with polio at another hospital. This delay in diagnosis had been costly. You cannot imagine how thin and deathly looking a person can be until he is right in front of you. When he looks into your eyes, an expression of utter despair accentuated by the gaze sunken into his small, sharply outlined, skull-shaped head, you have only two possible choices. You can either run or stay and help.

A particularly memorable case was a fourteen-year-old girl who was HIV positive. But she didn't just have HIV. She had full blown AIDS and also gastroenteritis, meningitis, and malaria. And no, there were no infectious disease specialists available for consultation. Even if there had been, there were few or none of the medications she needed in our pharmacy, assuming she or her family could afford it.

Somewhere around the halfway point of rounds, we interrupted our regularly scheduled program to take a lady from the women's ward to the operating room to perform a dilation and curettage (D&C). She had delivered a premature baby the previous night but she still had some retained placenta left inside and was slowly bleeding to death. The heat in the OR was so intense that the sweat poured off our arms and backs. I quickly lost all sympathy for the western surgeons who complain that a temperature of 72 degrees is too hot. The hottest it gets in Bere is about 130 degrees, and that is outside. I don't know how hot it gets in that concrete, tin-roofed box that served as an operating theatre. The first time I scrubbed in to assist James, I had to sit down four times because I nearly passed out. When we were finished that day, every area of my scrubs was soaked through with my own sweat.

This woman had been barely conscious before we took her to the OR, and she was hardly any better when we brought her back out. She remained unresponsive and was unable to breastfeed her premature infant. Because the woman's family refused to do so, Suzanne volunteered to manually milk the mother's breast into a cup so the baby could be spoon fed. Meanwhile, the wheezing sounds of labored gasps made me wonder if this woman would live past tomorrow. It was possible that she had an amniotic fluid embolism, but there was no way to prove it and no way to treat it, if that were the case. Whatever was wrong, if we lost the mother, the child would soon follow.

In between her episodic role of milkmaid, Suzanne also took turns taking another newborn outside into the sunshine for fifteen minutes every hour—the prescribed treatment for jaundice. The mother of this child was one of the casualties of the Arab cow wanders into rice field episode. She had been stabbed and wounded so badly, she was unable to care for her own baby. We expected the free UV therapy gradually to work its magic and that both mother and child would be okay, given sufficient time.

The pediatric ward was filled mostly with malaria cases although it was not the malaria high season. Late in the year, when the malaria cases peak, it is not unusual to treat more than twenty infants and children for the illness. On average, one in five lose their lives to the disease.

The men's ward had a couple of broken bones healing in casts, along with one interesting case that had been referred from the capital to James for evaluation. The long bone of the leg had been broken and set incorrectly (if at all) so that now the two pieces were healing side to side rather than end to end. This made the healed leg shorter than its counterpart. James re-broke the bone; set it with some pins, drilled through and through using a cordless drill; and held them in place with a length of PVC pipe at the side of the leg. He had to monitor the healing process without the advantage of X-rays. His hope was that after proper healing, the length of the broken leg would be closer to its original length and make walking more normal.

There was one other case in the isolation ward. I suppose the patient initially had been put there by hospital staff because they thought he had an infection that was affecting his brain or nervous system. Perhaps it was meningitis. But I didn't get the feeling that was his problem, and neither did James.

He was a very wiry, skinny guy, who ... well, he just wasn't quite right. When James and I arrived to check on the other patients in the room, this patient quickly took center stage. A small group of nursing aides tried to steady him and keep him from staggering off on his own as he lurched out in different directions. He was wild-eyed, wouldn't hold still, and fidgeted unpredictably by his bed. He wouldn't sit down, but he wouldn't stand up straight either. He either wouldn't or couldn't talk. At first glance, he had appeared weak, but as I watched he proved to be a whole lot stronger than he looked. He was of average height and could not have had more than ninety or one hundred pounds hung on his bony frame. The group of hospital workers tried to get him to lie down so that James could at least do a physical exam, but that was no use. As two of them got his legs off the ground, James and another assistant tried to guide his top half back onto on the mattress. The little guy deftly resisted everyone's combined efforts to subdue him and in the process nearly bench pressed the six-foot-tall James off the ground, using just his left arm while fighting off the other worker with the other. Everyone stepped back for a bit to take a breather.

I had read accounts of, and even spoken with, people who had first-hand encounters with people who either possessed or were possessed by supernatural powers. Depending on who you believe, the latter of those two possibilities is the only real option. But until now, I had not yet witnessed possession myself. For most Western minds, the idea of demon possession is confined strictly to the movies, fiction, and role-playing games. In much of the third world, though, it is a way of life. It is their religion. Since ancient times, nearly every major civilization has had structured, socially accepted relations with dark, supernatural powers. Egypt, Babylon, India, sub-Saharan African cultures, the Indian civilizations of Central and South America—all these have copious amounts of archaeological evidence recording dealings with the gods that people believed controlled every aspect of their lives, from war to weather, from farming to family planning.

James had encountered these beliefs a number of times among the people in Chad. Often, instead of operating or writing a prescription, he called for the chaplain, who had a special prayer service with the patient; he, too, suspected the man was possessed. The chaplain could (and probably should) write his own book describing his life experiences. Not the least interesting aspect to his life is how he used to be a very successful, Russian-trained, Muslim terrorist prior to his conversion to Christianity. He said he used to really like killing Americans. Anyway, to make a long story short, the patient was seated and in his right mind next time we came through; no other interventions were needed.

Across the hall, Suzanne helped care for the baby whose mother had been unconscious and unable to breast feed. Unfortunately, death had quietly come and taken the woman's life. The surviving newborn didn't have a chance. How could it? There was no neonatal intensive care. There was no nursery, no lactation consultants. There was no orphanage, no Child Protection Services. All that could be done had already been done. There are times when you must face the fact that your best was not good enough.

Exercise is always a great tension reliever, and so Suzanne and I tried to wind down from the whirlwind of a first day on the job by getting in a workout. For me, it was pushups and some work with a pair of resistance bands I had brought along. For her, it was sit-ups and a brief run around the hospital grounds. Of course she had to run in scrubs, because the locals consider it pornographic for women show their knees. The other option was a skirt, but she would have none of that.

And so at last, the first of a number of long hard days of work came to an end with a cool shower of well water. Though we were very fatigued and feeling a little sick, the two of us managed to scavenge for food—that first day all we had was bread for breakfast, beans and rice for lunch, and the locally made peanut butter on bread with a side of sliced tomatoes for dinner—and chat a bit about the next day's agenda before heading to bed. We planned to go on morning rounds, start an inventory of available medications and supplies, and then plan an order for all the medicine estimated to be required for the rest of the year. This would be a challenge because we knew that no one was keeping track of what was being used, or how frequently. The hospital's central supply operations were simple: when they have something they use it, and when they don't have something, they go without and try to find more (usually back in N'Djamena).

Of utmost importance, we would try to eat more calories. We planned to go on a mission to check for which fruit, if any, was in season at the market. We had already heard that yes, they had no bananas, for the rest of the year.

⚜

Things you don't want to hear in the mission field:
"Sure! I'd be glad to help you wash dishes, right after I finish going to the bathroom."

Rise 'n Shine

The next day Suzanne got up and ate porridge made of peanut butter, rice, rice milk and a touch of lime for breakfast. It actually was quite good. I had a glass of water, which was followed by the sudden desire to eat nothing else and go directly back to bed. But then they called for anesthesia help during an exploratory laparotomy for a large abdominal mass, hernia, and hydrocele. So I got out of bed anyway, skipped breakfast, and went to work. As we got into the case, we found an obvious intrahepatic tumor (cancer in his liver) that likely had spread from somewhere else. James felt the spleen and announced that he could feel some studding there that was likely metastasis. Bummer. An earlier ultrasound hadn't looked all that bad, but now it was apparent that we faced a bigger challenge than we had thought.

Obvious tumor involvement was apparent across the surface of the left lobe of his liver. A bleeding stink of a mess awaited us if James elected to attempt a partial liver resection, something usually only done by a liver transplant surgeon and an anesthesiologist who was equipped with double central lines, two dozen units of blood and clotting factors, and pressurized infusion devices to overcome the blood loss, which would occur at a rate of about one liter per minute. We checked the hemoglobin. It was 7.0, the lowest you usually let a patient go before transfusing and we hadn't even begun to work on the liver yet! What were we to do? If we continued, he could bleed to death. If we didn't, he certainly would die of cancer. We decided to let the family choose; they knew best what choice the patient would make if he were awake and aware of the situation.

After talking with James, the family decided that it would be best for us to close up his wound and let him have whatever quality of life he had left instead of taking the risk that he would bleed to death as we attempted to cut out his liver tumor. Unfortunately, I had hammered him with enough ketamine to keep him asleep for several more hours so it was quite awhile before he actually woke up to talk with us or his family.

Suzanne and I started an inventory of the anesthesia equipment and drugs as a way to start building a model for a hospital-wide system of tracking the use and acquisition of drugs. When we arrived, there were only two answers to the question of how much of any kind of drug or supply the hospital had. One was, "We have that." The other was, "We don't have that." For example, one day some of the workers told the administration, "We need to fill the generator with fuel today and that will leave us with an empty reserve tank." There was no mechanism by which to tell *when* to order more of *what*, and no one tracked the supplies that were used up during the day-to-day hospital operations. You can imagine the feeling you get when you discover that you are out of something important at the exact time you need it most. You've heard of doing things the "American way?" Well, that's how things are done the "African way."

While tossing ideas back and forth about these logistical problems, Suzanne and I went to market to look for flip-flops. I wanted a pair to walk around in so that I could get out of my closed shoes and socks. They would be much cooler and easier to change quickly into my surgery shoes when an emergency arose. So we went to the Bere market for the first time … alone. We walked along the path past chickens, goats, pigs, and cows, gradually getting closer to where we'd been told we'd find the market. Every so often we passed a group of children who would either greet us enthusiastically or flee in terror at the sight of us. It kind of felt like our first day at school. We didn't know anybody around us, didn't know exactly where to go, weren't sure what we'd find once we got there or whether we could find our way home at the end of the day. We spoke just a little French and a few words of Chadian Arabic. But we managed to find and buy flip-flops! We were so proud of ourselves and our little purchase, even though my plastic Chinese sandals were two sizes too big. But it was a start, and we felt encouraged that by our next trip we would be able to attempt more advanced transactions, which no doubt would include the nearly universal American phobia of bargaining.

As the heat of the day diminished around the covered stalls of the market, we managed to find our way back to the hospital grounds. We were parched with thirst and sticky with oily sweat and the unavoidable layer of dirt that accumulates on any exposed surface of skin. Others who had been there long-term suggested that the best way to stay clean and cool was to shower every chance you get, without using soap—that was saved for when you really meant business. You also had to watch out for little wounds on both your hands and your feet; they constantly get used and abused and can easily get infected with the most bizarre bacteria. And antibiotics can be hard to come by so prevention is much better than trying to get some cure.

Another thing that we had to incorporate into our daily mindset was that cooking had to be done on a continual basis because there was no refrigeration. Thus, if you wanted to eat something other than fruit or bread and peanut butter, first you had to find it, then you had to cook it—without electricity. You also had to remember to plan well enough ahead so you wouldn't have to go back to the market and buy any ingredients you'd forgotten to get the last time you went.

Cooking was done over charcoal stoves, which either were wire cone frames that sat inverted on the ground or stone/brick ovens with a hole into which the charcoal was loaded and lit before the pot was placed on top. This stuff was not the charcoal we'd seen in the States; it was made from small tree branches, not fuel-soaked briquettes. And let me tell you, it burns hot! We realized during the last communal cooking spree—hosted on our three stone stoves and two wire charcoal burners—that one really nice benefit of having concrete floors is that if and when you spill the hot coals all over the place, the house won't catch fire and burn to the ground around you. Genius!

Franklin V. Cobos II, MD

☙❧

Things you don't want to hear in the mission field:
"I've already had malaria *twice* since I got here! It's not that bad really. Well, except for those first two days."

A Day at the River

Finally, the weekend arrived and with it a much needed Sabbath rest. Everyone slept in, which meant we got up around 7:30 a.m., two hours after the sun began to rise and light up the windows. Everyone that is except Mr. Speckles, the rooster, nature's natural alarm clock. He seemed to take a certain amount of satanic satisfaction in stealing away the sleep I felt I deserved. I could tell, even at this early point in my life in Chad, that he and I would develop a very special relationship. And, if he were lucky, I would let him live in spite of it.

After taking a quick cold shower and eating breakfast consisting of left over porridge, bananas, and bread, Suzanne and I made our way over to the little mud-floored building where the surrounding community and the hospital workers had gathered for worship services. As the sun continued to rise higher and heat the sky, we walked across the hospital grounds, through the horse gate, and over the parched earth, arriving at the church located outside the hospital grounds. It turned out that during the first few hours or so everyone sang songs a cappella, all of which were in French, recalling the tunes from memory. There was no piano; however, there were a few drums and a mini tambourine, which I was handed unceremoniously and had to learn how to play on the fly. Evidently, they didn't understand that just because a white man comes to Africa doesn't mean he has any sense of rhythm or skill with percussion instruments. It was difficult to understand much of anything since the sermon, too, was in French and translated only into the local dialect. Wooden planks without backs or seat cushions served as the pews. I suspect that was by design because those seats made it harder to fall asleep in the sweltering heat.

After the service, everyone had a chance to eat something for lunch before gathering to make a trek to the river for a swim. Allegedly, this was to be a two mile walk or a short ride atop one of Sarah's two horses. Those who have ever been in a third-world country know that if a place is said to be two miles away or will take one hour to get there, what that really means is that it's closer to three to four miles away and will take at least two hours to get there. I thought that it wouldn't matter how far off the time estimate was since I was going to ride Bob. The problem, however, was that Bob liked to run. So I was constantly trying to hold him back by the reins before he built up enough momentum to leave me trailing behind him in the dust, dragged along on my back, with one foot and Chinese sandal wedged inside a stirrup. In addition, the harder I pulled back on the reins, the more the metal stirrups pressed into my bare shins. Truly, flip-flops are not the best for riding horseback.

Having endured and barely conquered Bob's urges to execute two wind sprints every three to four minutes, I arrived at the river in one piece without having fallen off. I oozed off of Bob's back, my fatigue worsened by the heat of the day. Along with the others, I slowly began to wade out into the refreshing current of the river. I must say it is kind of cool to swim in an African river. There's a sense of mystery, really: always wondering if piranhas will start eating you even though, intellectually, you know piranhas are only in South America. Still, your head plays games with you, saying things like, "they just might make it over here somehow. I mean, it's just the other side of the world. There's water between here and there. They can swim, you know."

The current was quite strong, and it took a while for a smaller group of us to swim to the other side. That side had several trees growing near the riverbank, one of which was just begging to be climbed. It was positioned perfectly for a jump out into the river from a sturdy branch located halfway up the tree. I don't think I had climbed a tree in more than twenty years and getting up to that branch was at least half the fun. Finally, after carefully climbing up with wet slippery feet on the smooth tree bark, I reached the spot that I had eyed as I swam across the river. I paused. Wow! What a feeling of freedom, standing there overlooking the river, watching it flow toward the horizon as it cut across the savannah. Perhaps it had something to do with the fact that there was no one yelling at me to get down before I hurt myself.

Frankly, I didn't really care if I did a cannonball, belly flop, or ye olde Nestea plunge. But then, realizing that personal airway management in a swift current in the middle of Africa would be more of a challenge than my poorly insured self wanted on a lazy afternoon, I decided just to step off the limb. Dismissing thoughts of freshwater alligators as I surfaced for air, I relaxed and let myself get swept downstream, then gently paddled back toward the other bank where the others were wading in the murky, brown water.

We stayed as long as we dared; we didn't want to risk too long of a walk back in the dark. The mistake I made was not taking into account that near the equator, the sun falls more steeply and quickly below the horizon than in America. I also decided against riding Bob back to the hospital. My shins weren't able to take any more punishment from the stirrups. Thus, the last forty-five minutes of the trip was made under starlight. Sounds romantic, doesn't it? The problem is, walking around in the dark is no small thing in rural Chad, even if you are in a group. And I wasn't. Thanks to those Chinese sandals, my feet were killing me, and I fell further and further behind, eventually losing the sight and sound of the people on the path in front of me. There were no signs or directions anywhere along the cobweb-like network of footpaths that crisscross this area of land. Why, oh, why, didn't I bring my GPS? (Because I thought they'd steal it from me in customs.) Fortunately, the only cell phone tower for hundreds and hundreds of miles around is near the hospital. After it gets dark, if you're close enough, you can see the three red lights on its side. I knew the general direction I should go to get back home, and it was just a matter of time before the tower would come into view. I just had to keep walking. And walking. And walking! The whole trip left all of us with several blisters on our feet, and questions about why we hadn't thought to invest in $3 worth of moleskin from Walgreens, and why on earth I had settled for that European size 43 set of flip-flops instead of looking much harder for some 41s.

As we wilted into the simple furniture in our quarters, our futile attempts at connecting to the Internet for email and blogging drained what little energy we had left. I turned on the shortwave radio I had brought, trying to get some small glimpse into what was going on outside our small, remote world. We didn't learn much. And with that, it was time for bed.

It was noticeably cooler at night in the southern part of the country compared with N'Djamena. Locals claimed that I would get accustomed to the heat, but I wasn't holding my breath. It was comfortable only between four and seven a.m. After that, you might as well just get up because you're soon going to get hot and sweaty anyway!

Franklin V. Cobos II, MD

☙❧

Things you don't want to hear in the mission field hospital on rounds:
"That guy doesn't look so good."

A Day at the Market

I knew it would happen, eventually. One day, we ran out of running water. So we had to start the generator, burning precious diesel fuel, to pump water up into the gravity feed water storage tanks. I had gotten so used to having reliable water since arriving less than a week earlier that I had forgotten that going without running water is the norm in rural places. The nice thing about water in Bere is that it's fresh, clean, well water. There are actually two water tables in this area, one above bedrock and one below. The hospital administrative and guest houses all have water supplied from below the bedrock. That way, there's no risk of contamination from the agricultural runoff or private sewage "systems." At this point, I'd neither had to use the water purifier I brought nor boil water, which really shortened the tedious time spent during the day to overcome the inconveniences of remote living.

One day, I went through the huge blue shipping container in front of the guest house, similar to those that sit on the back of train cars, stacked two high. I was looking for goodies among all the donated junk. I wasn't disappointed. I promptly found two colonoscopes and a light source, although I wasn't sure if they actually worked; anesthesia masks; and breathing circuits, the last were critical for building an anesthesia system. To my great disappointment, I found no draw-over vaporizers. Without them, I would not be able to give patients inhaled anesthesia during James's surgeries. But I did find some good, used surgical instruments—thank goodness, I thought to bring along a sharpener—and a vacuum extractor, for the obstetrical bun that doesn't want to pop out of the oven after its gestational age is done.

As I made multiple trips back in and out of the container, gathering up all the scavenged treasures, I got the feeling that this stuff had been sitting in this metal box under the 130-degree summer sun for a couple seasons. Later, James told me it had been about twelve seasons. All the way in the back of the cargo box, I found large pieces of equipment that were supposed to be used for drilling wells. The problem was no one there knew how to use it, and I couldn't find any instructions lying around either. Good grief, what a waste.

After I got sick of cutting into cardboard boxes with my Swiss Army knife and before sorting through the unlabeled, disorganized mess, Suzanne and I went to market to search for lemons and bananas. We found a block of soap that would last both of us the whole month, and do all our laundry, for the equivalent of eighty-five cents. It took a while, but we also located some cloth that Suzanne wanted to be used to make a custom-sewn dress. The ten yards of cloth, plus the tailor's fee, combined to a total of $30.

We discovered many other interesting things at the market, including the fact that VISA actually isn't everywhere you want to be. In fact, I am personally convinced that the less credit and the fewer banks, the better off a society is. I've not been able to find debt here. If you ask me, I think the world ought to just go back to bartering with gold and silver. People here are blissfully unaware of Western economies and really could care less what happens to them because by and large, they remain unaffected if banks fail or the stock market crashes.

In the process of making this foray into the markets we learned how to say shukran ("thank you" in Chadian Arabic) from the fabric salesman, who thankfully spoke a bit of English. We also learned that buying cell phone airtime can occur in one of two ways. One way is to program the minutes into your phone after purchasing a paper ticket with an amount of talk time printed on the front and a pass code on the back, covered up by a silver paste. You scrape the silver patch off, as if you were uncovering a Lotto number, and enter it into the phone after dialing the phone company. Now, I've done that before. It's quick and familiar. The other way is for some guy on the corner, sitting on a cardboard mat, to call your phone with his phone, programming yours with extra talk time in the process. This, of course, requires you to know your own phone number. Which I didn't. I mean, I'd never had to call me in Chad, Africa. I'd just arrived. Why would I need to call me? It didn't make sense. After all, like the wise saying goes, "no matter where you go in life, there you are." So, because there were no paper tickets available that day, we got no minutes. Imagine the "Soup Nazi" from *Seinfeld* saying, "no calls for you!" as with a scornful gesture, he ejects you from the line of hopeful people awaiting his coveted services. Ah, the disappointment.

Returning from the day's field trip, we passed through the gate in front of the Appel's house and saw that James and Jeremy had been working on the Toyota minivan, which hadn't been running very well of late. Apparently "someone" drove it through deep muddy water during rainy season and now not only was the battery dead, the starter was questionable as well. I had recharged the battery the night before with a charger I had brought from the States, but we still couldn't get the vehicle running without a push start. We knew that it wouldn't make the eight hour "road" trip to N'Djamena scheduled for the next day. We never would have been able to roll it out of the mud after getting stuck eight inches deep like we had on the way to Bere.

In the evening, we watched some people play soccer as the sun set beneath the African horizon, framed with flat-topped acacia trees growing up from the flat grassland. One of the most memorable sights I had on this trip was seeing a goalie who played his position on the soccer field while hobbling on one crutch. He was quite good, actually, and it was inspirational to watch him play. Though he never did, I couldn't tell for certain if it was illegal for him to use his crutch to prevent the opposing team from scoring a goal. Maybe he was afraid that people would accuse him of using it as a crutch. I wasn't sure. You'd think that it would only make sense to use a crutch *as a crutch*, right? But ethically, was it the right thing to do? Would you call it a hand ball? It's a tough call. Where's the referee, when you need him?

After it got too dark for me to enjoy watching the game, I went back to the guest quarters and built the charcoal fire for the ladies who got the food ready to make supper. Now, let me ask you a question: have you ever felt like you've been helped enough? Let me give you an example. One of the guys there felt I was using too little gasoline to fire up the little pieces of charcoal. I disagreed, didn't think I needed any help creating a conflagration for cooking, and purposely placed the one-liter plastic bottle of gasoline out of his reach and away from the hole that held the charcoal. That way, I could safely focus on fanning the growing embers through the little wind tunnel cut into the concrete and stone that lead to the fire pit portion of the "stove." As I vigorously flapped the dried grass fan in an attempt to get the fire started, my "helper" proceeded to add some fuel to the fire and relight the charcoal after placing the bottle of gasoline on the back side of the cooking space. A column of flames promptly shot out of the hole as if the afterburners of an F-14 had been ignited, reaching nearly to the ceiling. Although visually impressive, this sudden turn of events unfortunately cut off easy access to the bottle of gasoline he had just placed on the other side of this private inferno. I tried to put aside my anger for the moment and quickly thought about how I was going to get that bottle away from the fire. I grabbed the biggest pot I could find, covered the flames, and frantically reached across to grab the now-hot plastic bottle and move it to the other side of the cooking area, away from the flames, and away from my eager assistant. I didn't say *anything*, not even "thank you, I've been helped enough!"

At some point after all this excitement, I noticed that my shoes were missing. I cannot tell you how distressing this was. I'd bought them specifically for this trip and put orthotics in them to comfort my flat feet. I had only recently started wearing the cheap flip-flops and had left my lace-up shoes in the foyer of the guest house, across from the cooking "stove." That way, I could come and go more quickly, swap them out on the fly when entering the OR, and be cooler in general because my feet were bare (It also spared me from washing socks). "I swear," I muttered to myself, "These people with steal anything, from anybody, at anytime, for any reason! Drives me nuts." Stealing was so regular and predictable that James and Sarah politely turned down my gift of heirloom vegetable seeds, stating that they didn't garden because the food gets stolen before you get a chance to eat it yourself.

After washing my face as I got ready for bed, I realized there was one more issue I needed to work on. I loaded my toothpaste onto my toothbrush and let my mind wander as it looked for a solution the problem of the leaky and clogged sink and slow shower drain. As I brushed away the furry feeling that had accumulated around my teeth during the day, I listened to the water spill out of the poorly fitting P-trap pipe under the sink and out onto the bathroom floor, much of it missing the emesis basin we had placed there a few days ago to capture the water. It then dawned on me that the supplies I had brought to fix gas leaks in the anesthesia machine would work great for this problem, too.

I spent three hours trying to get the sink and shower to drain properly. I knew that Teflon tape and epoxy putty would come in handy. Silicon caulking would have been the best answer, but you use what you happen to have at hand. Before the ordeal was over, Jeremy and I had pulled out three rat-sized clumps of gooey hair and mud from the P-trap under the sink. This made the toilet plunger we used to clear the shower drain much more effective (both the sink and the shower drain into the same pipe system). Most important, a normal rate of drainage afforded us all the luxury of taking a shower without standing ankle deep in each other's soapy water runoff.

❦

Things you don't want to hear in the mission field:
"I geeve [give] you three peegs [pigs] and one cow to marry your cuzeen [cousin]."

Junk for Jesus

I awoke the next morning as the sunlight gradually lightened my room and shone through my permethrin-soaked mosquito net. I pulled out the earplugs I sleep with and right away noticed the unusual silence. "What a blessing!" I thought. "Maybe someone killed the rooster and ate him for breakfast. Ah well, God rest his soul. No, wait. God rest *my* soul, about another hour and a half, every morning." I glanced down at the foot of my bunk and saw that the battery-operated fan I had brought from the States had run out of juice sometime in the middle of the night. Yet even without it, I hadn't woken up to notice the irritable heat, which meant that the nights were getting cooler and hopefully would be easier to sleep through.

    I slipped out from under the net and sleepily shuffled across the hall to the bathroom and stood where the water that had leaked onto the floor had dried overnight. I washed my face and smiled at myself in the mirror, satisfied that I heard no leaking of the water like I had the night before. Score one for the expatriates. I walked back into my room to put on a fresh pair of scrubs and wondered how long my repair job would last. I hoped it would require no further attention because I had so much else to worry about besides trying to be a plumber.

After breakfast, we started the OR schedule, beginning with a simple hernia repair. Nice. I could do a spinal and not have to deal with the ketamine side effects for a change. James was pretty quick with a hernia repair so I could use lidocaine instead of the small, precious supply of bupivicaine that I planned to reserve for the longer surgeries. It surprised me that James used mesh to repair the many hernias people have here, rather than simply doing a primary repair with the patient's own tissue. The really interesting aspect of the repair is that the mesh is actually a small piece of a $10 mosquito net that is sterilized before use. It's a much more affordable way of creating a tension-free closure, and it's flexible enough to ease handling during placement. The same mesh technique is used in the States, but the material there is stiffer and more difficult to use, costs about $300 instead of ten cents, and people can sometimes feel them. So why don't we practice more rational and affordable medicine in America? My personal suspicion is that the reasons are largely political and financial.

As for the anesthesia, I did what I could with what was available. And, with James's translating, I was able to teach the French-speaking OR nurse some anesthesia knowledge that could be used even after I left. I planned to keep the training simple and limited to regional and ketamine anesthesia. If and when they are able to afford an anesthesia machine, I would consider returning to teach inhaled anesthesia. But for now, ketamine and spinals were affordable, effective, and most important, available. Those key features have kept James operating under difficult conditions for five years, and my job was to help the team understand these options inside and out and use them to their fullest potential.

Our second case of the day was a hysterectomy, which James said would take longer than the hernia. I used bupivicaine in hopes that it would last during the whole operation, provide excellent post-operative pain control, and avoid the troubles that sometimes occur when using ketamine alone. Part way through the procedure though, the patient started complaining of pain and really started to become uncooperative. It was a struggle to chemically restrain this lady, but a syringe full of valium, a touch of fentanyl and midazolam, a slug of ketamine, an ampoule of promethazine, another of chlorpromazine, and another syringe full of ketamine squirted up into her IV fluid bottle ... and viola! Things went much better after that.

I don't remember the next case. I mean, it's not like we kept an anesthesia record or anything. Paper was a luxury commodity in Bere, and even if we had kept records, they may have gotten lost or stolen. What was really memorable though was Suzanne's interjection of some very non-medical nomenclature into the operating room conversation. It happened as a group of us were in the pre-op holding area getting the patient ready for surgery. Jacob was starting the IV, Simeon mixed the pre-operative antibiotics and sedation, Abel prepared the instruments and surgical supplies while Jackson, Suzanne and I stood by, ready to roll the gurney through the double doors into the operating theatre. James was right there with us, seeing another patient who had come by for a post-op check following his testicular hernia repair a few days before. It was a simple chore for James; all he had to do was release the sutures. The man stepped into the room and following James's instructions, unabashedly dropped his drawers, and sat down right there on a stool across from him. James grabbed some scissors, and snip-snip ... that was it, sutures out, done deal. The patient pulled his pants back up, turned around, and away he went back out the door. With that brief delay over, we paraded through the double doors to begin the next operation. There were only two stools available for onlookers in the OR, and they were still warm from being freshly used. Suzanne, the only woman in the group, recoiled from the specter of having to use the second stool, grabbed the one James had been sitting on and brought it into the OR for her own use. Without stopping to think if she should use her *inner* voice, she bluntly announced, "I'm not sitting on that thing after he's had his nut sack all over it!" There was a sudden silence from the men in the room as they all slowly turned to look at who had just said that, accentuated by the stop-action suspension in what otherwise would have been a flurry of activity. I think it was the surgeon who broke the silence by saying, "Normally, we refer to it as the scrotum." We couldn't help busting up in laughter.

Our last case of the day was a woman with a huge fungating tumor on the bottom of her foot. As I looked more closely, I could see that it was actually several tumors merging into the larger mass that deformed her sole. It smelled like it had been there for months. Turned out, it had been. James actually had seen her about three months before, had taken off a small tumor from the foot, and referred her to her local health clinic for dressing changes. We doubted that she had gone for any dressing changes; otherwise she would have been referred back to us for removal of this huge mass that now was preventing her from walking. James performed a mid-foot amputation after I administered a lidocaine spinal. The main reason her tumor returned so quickly and aggressively probably was because she was HIV-positive. So, when Suzanne caught a bit of blood on her arm, she absolutely wigged out! It took me quite a bit of time to calm her down and assure her she wouldn't die from it and that HIV would not go through her skin. That's Karma. It's what happens when you don't use your inner voice for certain thoughts.

After we finished the surgical part of our day, Suzanne went to relieve her stress the way any woman on the planet would—by going shopping. I stuck around the hospital and brought out some of the donated surgical instruments for James that I'd found in the shipping container. He was very pleasantly surprised to see some of the things I had found in there, which he could use during surgeries. I was surprised that he was surprised. I mean, the container had been sitting there for three years. If it were me, I would have looked through the thing first chance I got.

We planned to have a little bit of Christmas together when both of us had a chance to go through the container. Most of what was sent over was absolute crap, actually worse than crap. If it were crap, we could have used it to supplement the charcoal. But we couldn't even burn most of the stuff. I am told that it is the exact same story at all of the mission hospitals in Africa, from Ethiopia to Malawi. Tons of medical garbage is sent over to these places in the name of "charitable donations." James had a different term for it. He called it "junk for Jesus," and I couldn't agree with him more. It's as if whenever people in Western medicine find themselves using undesirable instruments and materials they suddenly have some kind of wicked epiphany and want to give to Christ's cause the very things they themselves refuse to use. I imagine it as being kind of like the Life cereal commercial, just with two people in the OR commiserating over somebody's open abdomen, pulse oximeter chirping along in the background.

Surgeon: "#%*$&!! These scissors couldn't cut open a wet paper bag! And that needle driver is absolutely good for nothing, except driving me nuts!"

First Assistant: "Yeah, these are really bad. Why don't...."

Surgeon, interrupting: "How does anyone expect me to operate without decent instruments? Call the charge nurse! Get her in here! I demand that...."

First Assistant, interrupting: "Hey, hold up there, chief. Before you start throwing things again, I've got an idea ... yeah, I know. Let's give them to Jesus!"

Surgeon: "Great idea!"

First Assistant: "Yeah! He'll use *anything*!"

Surgeon: "Charge nurse! Put these and all the other pieces of crap I've thrown against the wall into a box and label it 'Donation for Africa.' And make sure we get a tax write-off for it too, eh? Thanks."

First Assistant: "Perfect! You know, you should throw things more often! No, wait. Just kidding."

Surgeon: "Anesthesia?! Go change the music on my new iPod to *Me Closing My Beautiful Incision*.

I hate those types of guys. I really do. They've turned Africa into a medical garbage dumping ground, and I was the one who had to wade through it all and sort out what was even remotely useful. Fortunately, I came prepared. I brought a sharpening tool, and those crappy scissors were nicely sharpened and ready for the charcoal-fired autoclave sterilization process the following day or that same night. I wasn't sure when they actually did it. It seemed a bit hot to fire the charcoal in the afternoon, when it was about 103 degrees Fahrenheit.

I actually saw a few patients in the ER/outpatient clinic. I couldn't believe it, me, an anesthesiologist seeing patients! It was weird. But it was necessary. Even with Michel, the French doctor who had arrived recently to temporarily bring some well deserved relief to James, we were nearly overwhelmed with work in the clinic. Anyway, my final patient of the day had diabetes, which was just as weird because in this area of the world people don't eat any processed foods. As James gave him his final instructions, I got a chance to evaluate him visually. He was an Arab with a long goatee extending from under the lower wrap of his turban and wore long sleeves and pants in 100-degree weather. He also was covered up halfway down to his knees in a winter parka with fur trim. (Picture Chevy Chase in *Spies Like Us*, minus the surrounding Siberian setting.) Then he and his buddy turned to head out the door after the perfunctory ritual goodbyes, handshakes, and "salaam aleikums." As he went to leave, he shook my hand, too. While I was discouraged because I hadn't understood a word he or anyone else has said during the entire conversation, I did my best to wish him well by waving goodbye with one hand, and dutifully shaking hands with the other while saying, "Better bundle up, it's kinda cold out there. Maybe consider adding some mittens to go with your parka, I don't know. It's up to you I suppose. Just a thought. Don't sweat it. Anyway, see ya!" Of course, he didn't get the joke. But I cracked myself up as well as every English speaker within earshot.

Things you don't want to hear in the mission field:
"No, the nearest place you can buy toilet paper is back in N'Djamena. You may have to use your left hand."

A Horse Is a Horse, of Course, of Course

I had not come to the other side of the planet expecting to do veterinary medicine. But I did come expecting the unexpected.

Sarah, James's Danish wife and lead nurse for the hospital, happened to love horses. And she owned two of them in Bere. One of them developed some kind of abscess on the inside of his right rear leg, just above the knee. For whatever reason, the royal "we" decided that I would be the one to lance the thing to drain out the puss. This unilateral decision, made with no representation, was accompanied by obsequious assurances that this was a "good horse" and that he would never kick me in the face as I stooped over with a sharp object to inflict pain without anesthesia during this endeavor, which was clearly out of my specialty. So after shaking my head and reaffirming to myself that, "this is Africa," I found a #11 blade in the OR and hesitantly made my way over to meet Sarah and Suzanne. They were in the brick stable tying the horse's front and rear left legs together, ostensibly so I could save face (literally). After saying a brief prayer and strategically placing my right shoulder against his flank, and pushing my neck against his right hip, I felt down his leg with my hands until I found the abscess. The horse kept trying to push his legs together, just like a three-year-old who was trying not to wet his pants before making it to the bathroom. After a minute or so of jockeying for position, I was able to sink the blade all the way to the hilt, and a pocket of pus popped out as soon as I stepped away from the danger zone. Humph, that was easy, I thought to myself.

Sarah was so grateful for my help that the next day, when the horse came back with a huge, gaping, bleeding wound on the extreme upper-inner, left-rear leg, who did she turn to? Exactly. Me. Fortunately, I was given the anesthesia duty while her husband, James, was cajoled into doing the sewing. Once again, we raided the OR for some equipment, paid the pharmacy for four grams of ketamine, forty mg of Valium (perhaps a bit much, but hey, it needed to be enough to anesthetize a horse) and about twelve million units of penicillin. I've never started an IV on a horse, and I wasn't about to learn. So I made Sarah give the shots IM (in the neck muscles). It took a while, but the horse did get drunkish, and six of us combined were able to tip him over onto the ground. Unfortunately, he fell operative side down, making James's job all the harder. We poured some diluted bleach over the wound to wash it out and soon realized that perhaps I hadn't used enough medicine to anesthetize a horse. It still required six people to hold the animal down and tie up his legs so that James wouldn't suffer four or five different kinds of facial fractures while sewing up the horse's ass. I irrigated the wound by squirting cleaning solution over James's shoulder—carefully using him as an unwitting shield for my own protection—and occasionally ventured near enough to cut the sutures with the kitchen scissors. (Finally, a pair that actually cut!)

Now if you think people come out of ketamine anesthesia in a bad way, you should see a horse do it. This thing wigged out! He ran in circles while laying on his side, scraping off the skin near his eye and down the sides of his knees as he scuffled around on the ground. We stuffed a towel as best we could under his head to keep the damage to minimum, but he fought so hard, it was nearly impossible to do a good job of it. Of course, the horse couldn't feel anything he was doing to himself and wouldn't stop doing it either. After about twenty-five minutes of this fiasco, enough of the medications wore off so the horse could actually stand up ... sort of. Good grief! I thought people were hard to deal with. Anyway, best we could guess, either a bull gored the thing from behind—unlikely, since it's a fast running horse; I should know, I rode it—a person threw a spear or knife while chasing it out of their garden or property, or it got spooked and backed into an old, stiff, half-cut palm frond sticking out of the base of a palm tree. Those things are vicious, like gladiator weapons!

I also anesthetized a human on that day, an eleven-year-old girl with a cleft lip that James did his best to fix. She really needed the operation, which would give her a chance at a normal life without ridicule and possibly marriage. My problem was that I couldn't put a breathing tube in this kid to protect her lungs from the bleeding that would occur from the mouth and lip. Her mouth just wouldn't open after we gave her valium and ketamine, and there were no inhaled anesthetics or muscle relaxants available. I considered injecting epinephrine around the surgical site to decrease the amount of blood running down into her airway, but James and I feared the tissue deformation would alter the appearance too much and interfere with the surgical repair. So I shot her IV bottle full of ketamine, set the drip rate by hand, put on sterile gloves, and suctioned as much blood as I could before it ran down into her lungs. Complicating the situation was the fact that all she had to breath was room air. Running too many things in the OR on generator power has been known to blow the generator, so the oxygen concentrator wasn't a reliable option when suction, overhead lights, pulse oximeter, blood pressure cuff, and the (excuse for) air conditioning were all running at the same time. It was a new kind of airway "management" for me. Before all was said and done, she'd lost about 200 ml of blood in the suction canister and we'd pulled out two very large, long clots from her posterior nasopharynx. Fortunately, she coughed up some blood a few times and that cleared out her airway almost as good as the suction did. I dripped some dilute epinephrine into the wound from time to time, and we held pressure on occasion, learning that it was true—all bleeding stops eventually. I left her laying on her side after surgery, after briefly considering holding her upside down by the ankles to see if I could drain out any extra blood. But since her blood's oxygen saturation hadn't ever been less than 94 percent on room air, I didn't think it would matter much. I left her alone to wake up gradually as the day wore on.

The next patient on schedule was a nine-month-old. However, the parents refused to pay for the procedure, and James required payment prior to operating on anyone. It was a policy that worked well. It kept the hospital financially viable and helped more people than was possible by giving away care while going bankrupt.

With time to spare, I tried to repair a Welch Allyn ProPaq monitor needed as a backup in the OR, to no avail. None of my attempts at diagnosis or treatment seemed to help. I would have to try to think of something different the next day. The new power supply I'd brought from the United States operated with the local 220 voltage, but the plug was U.S. style. And although the OR had U.S.-style plugs, they all were fed by a 110-volt circuit from a generator. So that would take some work. It was the old lead acid battery that had gone bad and broken the flow of electricity, even when it was plugged into a good power source. I planned to attempt to rewire it when I had more time. And, if it went "kablooey" when I turned it on, oh, well. It's not like it was successfully being used before.

Suzanne was to pick up her local garb the following day, too—she'd met the tailor for measurements two days earlier—and planned to buy some cloth for me as well. After some internal debate, I'd chosen to go Osama style ... turban and all. Suzanne insisted that she would get me a pair of gold aviator sunglasses to wear with the outfit as well as a pair of all-leather, Ali Habibi sandals with the thick strap that goes all the way around the big toe, which facilitates running from the local authorities. I could imagine myself landing in Omaha, Nebraska, all decked out like that and walking past security. Ha, ha!

Things you don't want to hear in the mission field:
"No way, it's way too long to be one of my hairs."

Things That Go Bump in the Night

One of the reasons people refer to the jungles of Africa is because of all the animals that live and move in, out, about and around here. Our encounters with animals provided various levels of entertainment for me and sheer terror for Suzanne. The first time was when a praying mantis landed on the broken screen window between us. I made an offhand comment about it, knowing Suzanne wanted to avoid all contact with creeping insects. She surprised me by grabbing her camera and snapping pictures right away. As she zoomed in on it, the thing turns its head and looks right at her with its alien-looking, triangle shaped head and shiny, silver, googly eyes. At that instant, she freaked out. She climbed over me, nearly trampling me as she fled the scene. And if that wasn't enough to fuel her paranoia, the big bats that whooshed by us the next evening while walking back to the house under the mango trees certainly were. I hadn't seen her stop cold in her tracks like that since we first arrived in N'Djamena and saw ten-inch lizards scurrying up and down the outside walls of our room.

Of course, that was just an introduction to the creepy, crawling wildlife with which we would share this experience. After we settled into our rooms at the hospital guest house, Suzanne was awakened one night by a scratching sensation under her bed. That would have been the mice or the rats. She told me the next morning she'd almost woke me up at 3:30 a.m. and told me to come into her room and kill whatever was living under her bed. I assured her she would get used to it, that I had heard it too, and that it was unlikely that they would chew through her mosquito net to come inside her bed. Oh, and let's not forget the two large spiders that lived under the pictures hanging over the dinner table; they would come out like clockwork each time we sat down to eat. Suzanne did finally accept those occurrences as facts of life. Still, one wasp did cause her to wig out one evening, flailing her arms wildly around her head, tripping and nearly collapsing on top of me and my laptop while I was trying to study my French. She really hated the insects here. Have I mentioned that yet? In fact, nothing gave her more joy than to hear the bug zapper *snap* in the evening as we sat around using iTunes to play *Name That '80s Tune* after dinner.

ఴఴ

Things you don't want to hear in the mission field over dinner:
"Oh, now I wouldn't go so far as to say there are actual rocks in the rice. Think of them as large pieces of sand. Beans though, they have rocks."

Step into the Sun

The previous five years that James had spent in Bere largely had been characterized by limited electricity. There was no "grid" there. There were four generators, two of which were broken beyond service, despite numerous previous repairs. Of the other two, one did run so the fresh water tank could be filled and running water restored to the hospital grounds (an every-other-day endeavor around here). To get it started, I went with Abel, the nearly deaf, Chadian surgical scrub tech, and Jacob, an American premed college student who was volunteering there. This is what I saw.

The generator looked as though it had been made circa 1920. Abel tried to explain to us, in French, how to start it, while Jacob and I tried to pretend we understood. An exceptionally large shaft stuck out of the front of this thing to which Abel attached a hand crank, very much like one on a Ford Model T. On top of the generator was a large slide switch that he talked about and moved from side to side as he made a circular cranking motion with his other hand while making put-put-put sounds with his lips. He hefted the crank around for a few seconds before he got tired and yelled something in French at us. Jacob tried throwing the switch and Abel stopped turning, but the engine just sputtered to a halt. Abel tried to explain again what we were supposed to do, and we did it all over again. This time he yelled something I understood, "C'est bon!" "It is good," I repeated in English to Jacob, who slid the lever again as Abel stepped back out of the way, and the motor slowly chugged to life. We smiled at each other and nodded heads in sync, gloating in a way that only men can, having achieved something so small yet so critically important.

James told me that that generator had been repaired by a pilot (long gone) nearly every other day for the past two months. It was a miracle the thing actually functioned at all, and it was quite expensive to run. The analysis I am doing will help James determine whether or not it would be in his best interest to purchase another 25-kilowatt generator or double the solar panel array.

The solar panels were a very recent addition, completed with a recent donation received just a few months earlier. Their addition has allowed the night shift to have lights in the hospital and the OR to run electrocautery (the device used to stop bleeding by generating small, controllable electrical burns), overhead lights, an air conditioner (well, sort of ... it's better than nothing!), suction, and patient monitors. The system also supplies a limited amount of electricity to the houses within the hospital compound. As a result I could charge and use my computer without pulling out my own 60-watt foldable panel to charge the battery pack. The computer links via Bluetooth™ to the Chinese iPhone clone, and from there, to the Internet. The phone is charged via a USB port when the computer has power, or via the handheld panels I brought for the iPod and iPhone. Neither of my solar systems had been absolutely necessary up to this point, which was kind of nice, but it did make me feel as if I'd carried extra weight for nothing.

I measured the solar array's maximum power output at 1.25 kilowatts when the sun was at its highest, though it dropped to about 750 watts about three hours either side of that time of day. Cumulative power storage for a day was about 8.5 kilowatts. We hoped to figure out the power draw of all the major appliances to determine whether to get more panels, more batteries, or both, or neither. The panels may have been conserving energy for no reason. They had a battery bank of twenty-four 2-volt batteries holding 900 amperes. The charge controller prevented more than a 50-percent discharge, to maximize the battery life, which was supposed to be about twelve to fifteen years. But that estimation did not account for the summer heat in Chad, which probably cut their lifespan in half, at the very least. Ideally, hospital staff ought to bury the batteries to keep them cool year round. The panels were quite dirty when I got to Bere. I cleaned them off and got about 10 percent more power the next day. Also they faced a bit too far west, and were lying too far on their backs. My next step was to redirect them so that they would more closely approximate a 90-degree angle with the sun around the local time of solar noon (11:30 a.m.). That gave them a bit more power too. Ten percent may not sound like much, but over a year's time, it would add up to more than an extra month's supply of solar energy, free of charge.

In between measurements, we played a card game and went shopping at the market, where we found fresh chai tea, sugar, limes, bananas, bread, and phone credits so we could send text messages and connect to the Internet. Suzanne tolerated one drunk suitor a little too long, allowing him to take his picture with her. Afterward, we agreed that next time I would be responsible for breaking up that kind of scenario, pronto. We passed the theater, which was a tiny area darkened by grass mats used as walls while American films subtitled in French were shown on portable DVD players. The cost was about 25 cents U.S. Curiously, it cost about the same to recharge a cell phone, which was done by the phone company. The phone company ran a large generator to power its tower, so it sold off the excess to people wanting to charge their cell phone; after all, most people had no electricity at home.

We saw a metal worker working with what looked like iron or steel. He had two hand bellows that he used to heat a small clump of red hot charcoal, then strike the hot metal in order to shape it into various tools (spear heads, knife blades). Rumor has it that the Arabs make a much better and more threatening sword, with a lot more style too.

The fish section of the market was in full swing, and it stank to high heaven. It really reeked. I've smelled some filthy, foul filth in my life, but this was the most, worst, baddest thing I have smelled in my entire life. (Did I mention it smelled bad?) I'm confident that Allah himself would have been nauseated by the stench. Maybe it wasn't just fish. The cumulative aromatic experience included healthy and unhealthy doses of animal excrement, feet, unwashed hair, armpits, and other sweaty body parts of the type that rub together when you walk. Imagine our dismay when we encountered two student missionaries from the hospital walking towards us munching on this oil-soaked, orange eel/fish-looking thing we had fervently avoided all day. They claimed they had watched the things get deep fried in front of them so that had to have killed anything dangerous. I just shook my head. I couldn't see the wisdom in such a course of action; must have been a double-dog dare or something. Suzanne vowed on the spot to be a vegetarian for the rest of her life. I'm sure that the last trip to the market helped her make this decision. The cow (maybe goat?) carcass and pile of bones that was stacked up on a table in a corner of the butcher's area, entirely covered with flies that took flight as we passed, probably sealed the deal.

After securing our purchases, we bid adieu to all the gawkers who'd never seen a white or tan person before as we scurried out of the fish market. "Smell ya later!"

All the kids liked to line up and point at us, saying "Nassara!" It translates loosely to "whitey," and is derived from the Arabic word for Christian. At first, it was almost endearing, but after about a dozen incidents, it just became downright annoying. It was like getting swarmed by the paparazzi or something. There also was an Arabic variant with a more precise meaning that translated as "Christian dog." I had yet to be called that one. To keep things friendly, when the occasional child repeatedly (five times, minimum) asks, in a thick Chadian accent, "Whass jour naime?" I usually tell them, "Nassara … Monsieur Nassara to you."

When we arrived back at the hospital, Sarah had returned from N'Djamena with more toilet paper, assorted edibles, and fabric (sans turban) for my Chadian outfit, which James's Arab tailor was to sew for me before I left for the states. It was a nice light-blue color.

After retreating from the filth of the market to our bathroom for my ritual wash, I experienced the misfortune of running out of water just as I got started. So I went to bed without a shower to wash the day's accumulation of oil and dirt from off my face (no small amount) and without brushing my teeth or being able to flush the toilet. I was just like all of God's other creatures out here on the nearly desert plain, I suppose.

Honestly, life could have been worse. In fact, it was in the next building over, about one hundred yards away. This was a TB isolation ward. In the next building over, pediatrics, one child died every day over the course of a week. Only four child patients remain. The next building is the main ward, where patients with AIDS, etc., are in isolation. I use the term isolation loosely because the area is right next to the labor and delivery room. It was there that I helped James as he used lidocaine to anesthetize the ligaments that join a woman's left and right pelvic bones in the front, and then cut them in half to increase the diameter of the birth canal so she could deliver her baby before her contractions ruptured the recent C-section scar on her uterus. That way, she wouldn't bleed to death during labor as do many other young mothers in Bere. So, no, I didn't have running water or air conditioning. Yes, I smelled bad, and my teeth felt fuzzy, but things could be worse.

In fact, I slept well. I woke up the next morning to the sound of the generator and took a nice, cool shower ten minutes later, feeling really, really good to be alive. I suspected it had something to do with the simplicity and clarity of life in Chad. You get up because you wake up, not because the alarm clock goes off. There's little food so you eat to live, not for sport. There are no banks and no credit, so you buy only what you need and make the things you must have but cannot buy. You laugh every chance you get and smile at strangers because it's the only thing you know how to say. If you get angry, you can show it without worrying about going to anger-management classes. You cry bitterly because when you have so little, every loss is great. You have to live honorably and are wary of those who don't because there is no law and no law enforcement. And at the end of the day, you fall fast asleep because it's hard enough for you to survive, let alone help someone else to survive.

❦

Things you don't want to hear in the mission field:
"Dude, life is too short to need insurance. Besides, if you're sick enough to actually need medical evacuation, you're probably not going to make it out in time anyway."

What's Cookin', Doc?

Usually, we had a cook. Now, that was not as nice as it sounds. That's because the cook worked Monday through Friday, and only made one meal a day; after all, the entire nation was accustomed to eating once a day. I didn't take to that so well, as I can eat up to six times a day. So that was harsh for me, especially on the weekends. One day, we were essentially out of food (except for eggs); we had to go to the market to buy what we wanted and then return to cook it ourselves. it sounds easy; it wasn't. The process took approximately two and a half hours— a huge chunk of time out of the middle of what otherwise could've been a much more productive day.

We had to take back packs to the market; otherwise we didn't have enough hands to carry all the little individual bags of purchased items from the various vendors from whom we bought and bartered. Some provided plastic bags, but they often spontaneously tore apart halfway home, spilling our precious food out onto the footpath (frequently, on top of several little goat turds). But we couldn't count on vendors having even those flimsy bags. We had to go to the market on foot since, even if the hospital vehicles were working (and they often were not), gasoline was too expensive to justify the trip. It was about fifteen minutes each way (if no one tried to buy or marry your cousin). Once we returned, after running through the gauntlet of the Nassara paparazzi, we had to decide if and how to clean the food before attempting to eat it. Bananas were easy: unwrap with one hand, eat with the other. Packaged food (like pasta) was also easy. Tomatoes and lemons were tricky. Trust me, if you saw the hands that sold me this food, you'd question whether it was safe to eat. We decided to scramble the eggs on this particular day, along with some fried potatoes, tomatoes, and onions. Of course, that required heat, which leads to a more complete description of the stove.

The "stove" was a concrete-block, cookout-looking area that was screened in on the front side of the guest house. There were three holes on the cooking surface, slightly larger than the average cooking pot, each with two short pieces of iron rebar that could be placed across the opening to support the pot without preventing air from circulating from underneath, where the charcoal burned. The charcoal was loaded from the top, resting on three to four pieces of rebar built into the cement block in grill-like formation. This allowed the ashes to be removed periodically as well as provide a channel to fan the coals from the front opening in order to make them burn hotter. That was the temperature control: you, your arm, and a woven grass fan. As alluded to previously, the charcoal was easier to light if you used a little gas (emphasis on the word "little"). If too much was used, flames shot out from both the top and front of the stove, scorching eyebrows and burning knees. After it was lit and the explosive phase had passed, you had to kick in the action with the hand-held fan before the fire burned out and decide whether to risk adding more gasoline onto hot, yet barely burning, coals. (Let the official record show that I recommend against this approach.) I just fanned like a madman with one hand while putting in more charcoal with the other, as much as the growing fire could handle. At some point, the girls would call from the next room, saying they're ready to put pots and pans on the stove. Then, the often futile attempt at temperature control would begin.

On this day, however, this period was interrupted by a pop and a scream from the kitchen area, where the newly arrived Danish girl had been cracking eggs to add to our potato-omelet mix. I peered around the corner to see what was the matter. Things looked fine from where I was. I walked through the door and over toward her to see if she was as OK as she'd looked at first. And then, it hit me. The smell. Remember how I'd said that the fish market had the most, worst, baddest thing I have ever smelled in my entire life? Well, I spoke too soon.

The pop I'd heard was a small gaseous explosion that occurred when she cracked one of the eggs. The odor emanating from the blue goo with black speckles that covered a small portion of the countertop was physically overpowering. I'm talking DEFCON level-five biohazard here! There is no question in my mind this small capsule of supreme satanic evil could have been easily used as a weapon of mass destruction. Before we finished preparing lunch, we had "found" three of those little jewels. The last one contained a fully developed chick. None of us will be able to eat eggs again without thinking of that day.

After we had eaten and because we couldn't imagine smelling anything worse, Henry and I set ourselves to work on the bathroom plumbing. We poured boiling water down the drains of the sink and the shower, in hopes that it would dissolve the accumulated gunk, hair, oil, dead skin, soap, dirt and muck of the past decades that was slowing the water flow. It actually helped a bit, but what I would have given for just one cup of Liquid Drano. It would have been worth its weight in gold.

After we finished that chore and once the dinner plates had been cleared, I turned the table into a workbench and swapped out the sealed lead acid battery from the non-functioning ProPaq monitor, using the battery from the one good device the OR was using. It worked. Now all I needed to do was figure out if the charge controller was out or if the battery itself, if replaced, would solve the problem. James also suggested I try to get a second oxygen concentrator working, as a backup. I asked him how high a priority it was, and he shrugged. Truth be told, in over five years he never had anyone die because they didn't get extra oxygen. "It would be nice to have though," he said.

Suzanne had slowed down a bit, and even more so in the evening with a bad headache and stomachache. I hope it's not malaria. She hopes it's not malaria. James bet her all the Milky Way chocolate bars that she brought him from the United States that it was. We had to wait to see who was right, and who would win the bet.

We watched the sun set over the African plain while sitting on top of the water tower. It was really impressive. The reddish orange ball of heat quickly sank behind the flat-topped acacia trees that occasionally grow across the wide grassland, as we listened to the mooing cows come home. The stored heat of the metal water tank kept us warm as we sat in the twilight, cross-legged, staring out at the landscape. Smoke from cooking fires rose from the grass rooflines of the houses north of the hospital. It was nice not to have to do or think anything for a little while.

Almost as an afterthought, in the dusk of the evening we lifted the lid and peered inside to see just how much water was left in the tank for us to drink and take showers at the end of a long day. It was only about one inch full! There had been so many volunteers that the water tower had to be filled every day, instead of every other day. We rushed home to fill one large cooking pot and an emesis basin with fresh water so that we could take bucket baths when the water ran out. Fortunately, I had enough water to get a shower. I hadn't had one in two days.

—

Things you don't want to hear in the mission field:
"Oh, don't worry, the five-second rule applies here too."

Back to Market

My feet were swollen and hurting, which was not surprising since I'd spent over a week going barefoot and standing on concrete floors sans Ecco shoes and orthotics. (I really hate thieves.) While she knew this, Suzanne (still not feeling so well) insisted that I go with her to market so she wouldn't have to go alone. So, I did.

We were learning more about where things were. We found a guy who had a refrigerator—we knew of only two in the whole town—and sold powdered milk. His name was Mahamet Samir. He also had these unbelievably lip-smacking-tastic sesame seed snacks from Egypt. Around the corner from his shop were the baker's stalls with open, mud-brick ovens. Good stuff. While we were there, a guy from the next stall tried desperately to sell me some really dirty, ugly roots of some kind. He was the one and only guy I had ever seen smoking there. I didn't entirely understand his French, and he clearly didn't understand when I said that I didn't need any roots, thank you. Contrary to anything Nancy Reagan might suggest, it turned out you should never "just say no" because it is perceived as very offensive to reject someone else's goods. So I learned to say "I don't need any, thank you." I had just finished a cold drink in an aluminum can from Mahatmet's fridge, so I told him plainly and quickly in English (which of course, he didn't understand at all), "I tell ya what, buddy, I'm gonna just give you this can so you can use it as an ashtray. Would you like that?" "Oui," he said. So I handed him the can and tried to force his hand, holding his cigarette, to tap his long ash into the hole from which I was just drinking. He didn't get it. Everyone else around him seemed to, though, and they laughed at him.

After paying about 65 cents for three small round loaves of bread, we cut through a few buildings (i.e., brick, walled shacks), where the tailors ran their foot-powered Singer® sewing machines circa 1890. They'd been conspicuously absent for a few days, and we learned that was because, as a group, they'd refused to pay the marketplace tax. The police were looking for them, and they knew it, so they had been hiding out who knows where until the local version of the Super Fuzz had gone away. With the tailors nowhere to be found, we decided to stop and talk with the Arab cloth salesman who had sold Suzanne her cloth for her dress and also sold amazingly good tea). Using some English, some French, and a bit of Arab, I told him I had cloth and wanted an Arab tailor to make me a traditional pair of clothes in a very specific style, accompanied by a turban, not a cap. He told me to come back tomorrow afternoon (a common and predictable request) for measurements, and that the turban would be available in one week. Uh-huh, I thought, yeah, a likely story.

As always, the walk to and from market was punctuated by voices calling out "Nassara!" as we passed by. It occurred to us that if the situation had been reversed, we could never get away with what these people were doing to us. Imagine, a couple of white Americans out somewhere just minding their own business in San Francisco or Atlanta when these two guys from Africa walk past. They have just arrived and really only know a few words of English. One American jabs his arm and hand out like a knife as he repeatedly points towards the Africans and calls out loudly for all around to hear, "Blackie! Blackie!" That would never, ever be tolerated. But here in Africa, doing the reverse is perfectly okay. People could call me "Honkey," "Cracker," "Nassara"—they were all the same thing. Curiously, all the village kids called Suzanne's skin color "red." They paused a bit when asked about mine and still called me white. I couldn't help it. I was taking doxycycline as malaria prophylaxis, and one tends to get a monster sunburn after just a little sun exposure while on that medication.

CR ʂƆ

Things you don't want to hear in the mission field:
"Hey, Cobos! Are those your shoes that the goalkeeper is wearing?"

Malaria Strikes

Remember Suzanne's bet with James for the Milky Way bars? She lost. She had malaria.

It became obvious when she had both a headache and really bad muscle aches in both of her triceps, muscles she hadn't really used that much since we'd arrived. The fatigue confused the diagnosis a bit, since lack of food combined with the heat makes one tired all the time anyway. But she was more tired than usual, that's for sure. Add a little nausea to the muscle aches, though, and viola ... you've probably got malaria. We didn't even bother to check her blood smear, we just started therapy. She hadn't started vomiting yet, so I didn't have to start an IV for her quinine; she could just take the pills. In Chad, quinine therapy was combined with Doxycycline. Suzanne had to struggle to keep eating, though, since the quinine took away most of her appetite. But if she didn't eat, the quinine would make her hypoglycemic. It also made her ears ring in a high and highly annoying pitch. It got bad enough to make it hard to sleep at night sometimes and difficult to hear a conversation under certain circumstances.

The first night she was miserable. She was restless, had fever alternating with chills, and a bit of nausea, but mostly she just felt awful all over. Fortunately, I'd made her start medication earlier that day (over dosed her a bit with the Doxycycline as a means of revenge on the malaria parasites), and the next day she was feeling much better. On the upside, after a week of quinine, three weeks of sit-ups, and just as long eating only two meals a day, she'd lost two inches around her waist and could fit easily into her "skinny jeans." James claimed he could turn the hospital into a program for any American who has ever struggled with weight loss.

I continued to be well without even a case of traveler's diarrhea, although I admit that the cigarette smoke, first in Paris and then in N'Djamena, gave me a bad case of sinusitis. I got a few mosquito bites, but I took my low dose Doxycycline prophylaxis faithfully and had managed to maintain fourteen weeks of malaria-free life in Africa.

We continued to be busy in the operating room, usually seeing two to four cases each weekday. One day the nurses brought in an Arab woman who smelled extremely good but had an unusual problem. As best as we could tell, she'd been unable to get pregnant by her relatively older husband; remember, the average life expectancy in Chad is 41. She'd been pregnant recently but had lost the child and had been unable to get pregnant again since. We prepared her for her exam and probable D&C. It quickly became apparent that she was not going to let four strangers, all men, uncover her in preparation for the procedure. Of course, unless she was buck naked in a certain specific and strategic area, there was nothing we would be able to do for her. She thrashed around a bit, enough to make us feel like we were forcing her against her will (even though she'd already agreed to the procedure), and we gave up for the moment, not sure what to do or say (in Arabic, which none of us spoke). I figured it was time for a little better living through chemistry. After 15 mg of Valium, not only did she not care that she looked like how Allah originally made her, she would not remember the four men who were with her instead of her husband.

It turned out that her cervix was about as uptight as she was, and it took James twenty minutes of dilation before we convinced ourselves that she was no longer impregnable. We rolled her out of the OR and were promptly met by her devout husband, who covered her from head to toe. In his limited Arabic, James explained that "The door of the house of the child [i.e., uterus] was shut. I opened it. May Allah give you many children." The man looked very relieved. Later, when he passed me on the path, he paused to speak with me and taught me the typical Islamic greeting "Salaam aleikum," (Peace be with you) and its customary response, "Aleikum asalaam" (And peace be with you).

After settling into the guest house later that day, I was summoned by one of the student missionaries. A baby had been admitted with severe malaria, but the nurses couldn't successfully start an IV to rehydrate the child and start quinine. I quickly went to the Peds ward to see what I could do. We found the child, lifeless on the ground outside the entrance to the pediatrics wing, the mother weeping bitterly over her as the father covered the tiny body with a drape. She had been brought in twenty minutes earlier, and I wondered, yet again, why people wait until the last possible minute to take action. The more important it is to do something, the longer people wait to actually do it. I circled around the ward to see if there was anything else I could do before heading home. When I walked past the doorway again, the family was gone. A little wrist bracelet, so commonplace on the children, remained on the dirty concrete where the family had been. I stooped to pick it up and slowly stood, looking for the parents. I never saw them again and have kept the bracelet as a reminder not to put off the important things in life.

Not long afterward, I got another call about a similar problem. Same story, though this time the parents had come in earlier in the course of the disease. Everybody had tried to get an IV into this kid and had blown all the best veins. (I'd thought that only happened in the United States.) I tried a few places where I imagined veins to be, until I was convinced they were all mirages. I gave up, and went to the OR to get a 20 gauge IV catheter to insert blindly into the relatively large femoral vein. No sterile prep, no drape, no lidocaine, nothing except gloves (which the parents had to buy) and some alcohol sprayed on the skin. I felt for the weakly pulsing artery, knowing that the vein would be right next to it. I protected the artery with one finger, then took the catheter mounted on a syringe in the other hand, knowing that if I accidentally hit the femoral artery instead of the vein, all thirteen red blood cells left in this already anemic child would flow out on the bed. I said a prayer, and then slipped it right in. I stitched the IV onto the leg, covered it with a Tegaderm dressing to keep the flies off, made sure the quinine was ordered and that the blood transfusion was dripping. As I turned to go, I wondered how long the parents would keep the thing working; nursing care for each patient is largely provided by family members, since the one nurse has to cover the entire ward.

I didn't have to wait long to find out. I got called back to the ward that very night because the IV wasn't working. I went to take a look. The dressing I had so carefully placed was partially pulled back, and a fly was crawling on the bloody joint where the IV tubing joined the catheter. "Nice," I thought. There was dried blood and feeding flies on the tape I'd used earlier to secure the line to the leg and prevent any unnecessary tension on the connection. I did that on purpose because there were no screw-on type Leur lock connections here; everything was slip tip, making it exceptionally easy for IV sets to come apart. This was by design, as there were no such things as three-way stop cocks that would otherwise allow IV injections to be made without disconnecting the IV drip set tubing. To uninitiated eyes, the filth and lack of care and cleanliness was simply revolting. But, that's just the way life is here. Patients, and people in general, survive, live, and at times thrive in this dirty world. They have to. Or else they do not live at all.

I took off the Tegaderm dressing, pulled the catheter back a bit, got it running again, redressed it, and went back home to go to bed. I was glad to see that in the morning, the blood transfusion had been completed, and there was enough fluid in those little veins so that another IV could be started since my femoral line had been removed after it "quit working" (or something, who knows the truth).

附

Things you don't want to hear in the mission field:
"What's your blood type?"

Cat on a Hot Tin Roof

It was bound to happen. I mean, I had expected it eventually, just not so soon. Isn't that the way it tends to go? We finally got a case that was going to be very hard to do with the few anesthesia drugs and supplies that I had. I just hadn't spent much time thinking about what specifically I'd do for workarounds since I didn't have inhaled anesthetics.

James called me in to look at an abdominal ultrasound he was performing on a man with complaints of right-upper-quadrant pain. It seemed obvious, even to an anesthesiologist, that the guy had some junk in his gallbladder and probably needed it removed. The thing was, he was doing pretty well otherwise and happened to be the chief of the area. You hate to do something for a VIP and things go wrong, you know? But it seemed as though this guy's time had come. So after James made the decision to operate, I was left to figure out how best to do the anesthesia.

Ketamine and spinals were all I had, although after using nothing else for more than two weeks, I had gotten used to them and didn't mind the limitations all that much. On the other hand, James and I had not had to operate this high in the abdomen yet, so a spinal would probably not reach high enough to cover the operative area with pain control and muscle relaxation. Then again, ketamine, while entirely adequate for keeping the patient pain free and unaware of what was going on, likely would leave James a very difficult operation to perform, high up under the liver near the right lung and diaphragm, with no abdominal relaxation. What to do?

With few options, I chose an unorthodox approach. I planned to administer a spinal anesthetic, then tilt the table to get it to rise higher in the abdomen than usual. We avoid this so called "high spinal" under normal circumstances because the higher up the spinal cord the anesthetic goes, the more likely you are to drop the blood pressure, stop the heart, or weaken the patient's ability to breathe (big points off for the last two mistakes). It would be a bit of a trick, but if it worked, it would be just what the doctors ordered. The patient paid his bill, and we went to the OR to take care of business.

The spinal went in easily, and I slanted the operating table with the head down at an angle of about five to ten degrees for ten minutes while the spinal medication set in. His blood pressure and heart rate seemed to be doing fine, so we started the case. He didn't flinch at all as James cut him open and started moving toward the liver and gallbladder.

It took a while, but he did develop very low blood pressure... about 60/35, which is only half the normal value. Gulp. "OK, not a problem. I'm ready for this," I thought. I had some epinephrine set aside just for the occasion. I had jealously guarded it since my arrival because it was the only vial in the whole hospital. And I was about to need it. Sorely.

I got the sense that things weren't going to go as planned right after I cracked opened the vial. See, over there, most meds come in breakable glass ampoules. No big deal; many in the States do, too. You just crack the top off the vial; I've done it a hundred times (and only cut myself once). Well, this was a different kind of glass vial. This was a brittle, brown glass that shattered between my thumb and forefinger as I opened it, cutting my thumb and spilling out the precious fluid like perfume out of an alabaster box.

It was hard to stay calm in a situation like that. How much worse could it get? And the fact that I was the one who had essentially wasted the very drug that I desperately needed only made things worse in my racing mind. I muttered under my breath as I looked at the crumbled glass in my hands but noticed one larger piece of glass that still had a small puddle of epinephrine in it. It looked to be about one-twentieth of what had been in the vial. "Well," I thought, "it's all I've got, and it may just be enough." I just hoped that I wouldn't need the whole vial.

So I sucked it up and diluted the epinephrine with saline a ten-ml syringe, hoping that I wasn't inadvertently including any tiny broken shards of glass or trace amounts of my own blood. As I frantically tried to get the epinephrine ready, the automatic blood pressure cuff cycled again, and this next measurement was enough to convince me that there was no error; he really, truly, absolutely, positively was hypotensive. Worse, he wasn't responding in quite the same way to my voice or when I tapped on his forehead like he had been before. "Peachy," I thought. "Why does it always have to happen to a VIP anyway?" I kept working in a bit of God's vasopressor, one milliliter at a time. It took a few doses, but I was able to get him back up closer to 100/60 mm Hg, and he started to look a little more alert, even though he couldn't speak to me in my own language. It was enough to perfuse his brain with blood and he became responsive.

By now, James had been working for a while and was convinced his gallbladder was fine. That was good news for me. It meant that we'd finish quicker than I'd thought and that the spinal would not likely wear off before we finished and were on our way to the medical ward, where this patient would recover.

As James was wondering aloud how he could have thought things were so bad during the ultrasound examination, when in reality the gallbladder was pretty normal, he noticed a dark spot that seemed out of place. It was a little past the stomach, on the small intestine. Closer inspection revealed a duodenal ulceration that probably was the source of his upper abdominal pain, and it perforated while James was looking at it. We were stunned. We had operated for the wrong reasons, through an incision in a different place, using an anesthetic plan that would have been completely different had we actually known with what we were dealing. Yet, providentially, it worked out perfectly. James quickly fixed the defect, sewed on a patch of intestinal fat, sutured him up, and we wheeled him off to the medical ward for an uneventful recovery. It was amazing, just amazing.

I tried to do other stuff to help out around the hospital when we weren't actually operating. One day I planned to solve one problematic aspect of the water supply. A water tank, mounted above the garage, was filled via generator-powered pump that drew water from a well 300 feet deep. It was a very important feature of the hospital's operations. The water came from below the bedrock, so there was no runoff contamination. It was pure; there was no need to boil or filter it. The tank supply was used for nearly everything, from scrubbing up for an operation (important) to the patients' laundry and cooking (less important). It would have been nice if the surface water from the well (only about ten feet deep) was used for the latter since cooking always entailed boiling, and Giardia parasites on your clothes was really no big deal, especially since they would get cooked in the sun as the clothes air dried on the line anyway. But people being people, they would rather turn a spigot instead of draw from a well. So we ran out of tank water relatively often, and often it was at a very inconvenient time, such as the time to scrub for surgery.

The problem is that we never knew how much water was in the tank. We also didn't know if it was time to turn off the generator before wasting fuel as the overflow valve let excess water spill out of the tank after it had been filled to capacity by the pump. So I designed a gauge for the tank, MacGyver-style (modified from a similar design from an episode in season one of the T.V. show). I tied some fishing line to a plastic soda bottle containing about 50 ml of water and floated it inside the water tank. I fed the free end out a small hole in the top of the tank, near the edge that faced the hospital, and covered the edge of the hole with scrap plastic and epoxy putty I'd brought from the States. This way, the heat and friction would not cut or melt the line. From there, I ran the line down the side of the tank, back up again, and down once more, weighting it down with small lead sinkers on the free end. I had cut off several of the plastic rings from which the IV fluid bottles hang to make a pulley system, then cemented it onto the side of the water tank with more epoxy putty. The down, up, down arrangement of the line resulted in the middle third of the fishing line rising and falling with the bottle floating level with the water inside the tank. And for the finishing touch, I used a piece of duct tape as a marker to show where the water level was on the inside of the tank.

At least, that was my plan. When I actually climbed up on top of the garage to install this contraption, things got a little dicey. I took off my sandals (shoes had been stolen, remember?) to make it up the round-rung ladder that led up the side of the water tower. As I stepped off the ladder and onto the top edge of the water tower, my feet were scorched by the intense heat of the metal tank under the blistering Sahara sun. I instinctively lunged forward, away from the edge while hopping around toward the middle of the tower, just in case I lost my balance and fell over (at which point I fully expected to get second-degree burns on my hands and forearms). I very quickly realized that I was not going to be able to do this indefinitely. It must have looked like I was doing the samba, dancing around on top of what felt like the trap door to hell itself. Then I had another one of my brilliant ideas; I'd just sit down. After all, scrubs covered my legs. I'd have a little insulation and a bit of a reprieve ... just what the doctor ordered!

I quickly sat down and flopped my legs over the side of the tank, only to become acutely aware of the near moral imperative to "turn the other cheek." Buns burning, I maneuvered as best I could to relieve the only slightly diminished pain and heat coming off the top of the tank that had so recently been felt by my feet and now affected my rear. Clearly, that morning I had made the right decision to wear underwear instead of going commando; fortunately for me, I'd done laundry the day before. In the end, that little extra bit of insulation saved me from developing what I imagined at that moment to be lifelong, disfiguring scars all over my thighs and buttocks.

I somehow managed to "walk" my way over to the ladder without giving myself a smoking hot, wedgie-of-a-lifetime; scampered down to the cool, shaded underside of the tank; and put my sandals back on. I slowly hobbled away with a stout resolve to return only after the sun had set to complete my best laid plans, which, it turned out, worked perfectly.

Things you don't want to hear in the mission field:
"Yes, rice again."

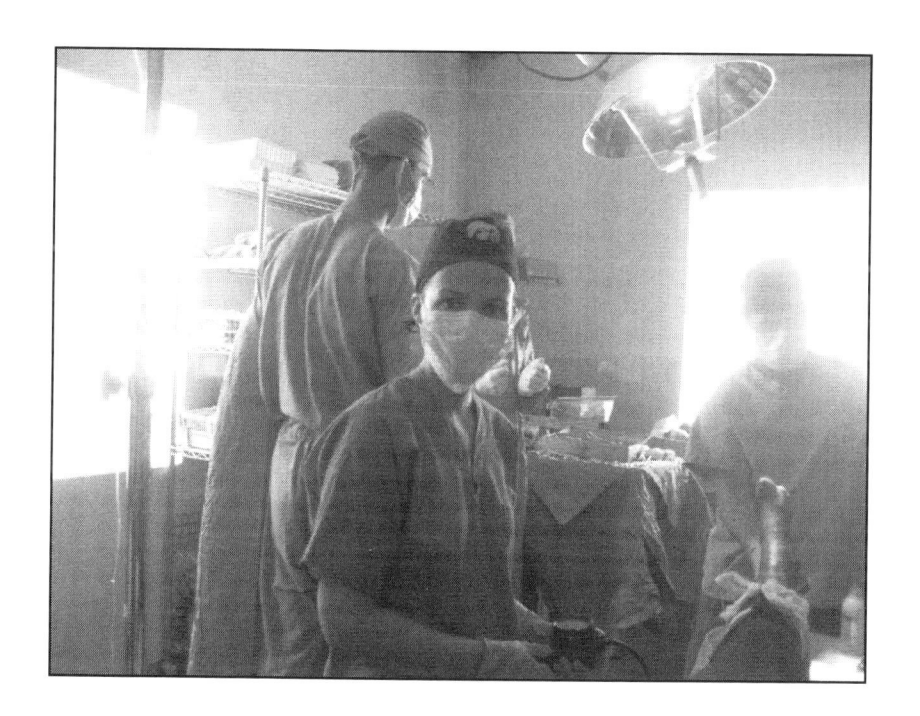

Things That Bleed in the Night

The month-long trip was almost over, and strangely, I still hadn't been woken up in the middle of the night for any emergencies. Until tonight, that is, at 4:30 a.m.

I don't remember much until I got to the hospital, which was only about fifty yards away from the guest house where I was sleeping. I'd been woken by a hushed, anxious voice calling to me from the darkness outside my screened window. I was needed at the hospital right away.

As I staggered through the door, adjusting my headlight and rubbing my eyes, I wondered what it could be. Whatever it was, it was probably pretty bad. Emergencies in Africa usually are. People usually get killed or die before making it to medical care or, by some miracle, actually survive but present doctors with some horrendous problem that is a) something they only heard about in medical school, b) saw once on The Learning Channel's *Trauma: Life in the E.R.,* or c) could easily be published as a case report in a leading Western medical journal.

I picked up the pace and rushed over to the labor room, where I could hear voices, and met a few people scurrying in there. As I came into the light, my gaze fell upon a woman; I knew immediately that she was in trouble. I can't remember if I said it out loud or not, but all I could think was, "She doesn't look so good." Her eyes were partially rolled back in her head, she was gasping for air, weakly and infrequently, and lying in a puddle of her own blood. Her skinny abdomen was grossly misshapen considering that it should have contained an average, round, five- to six-pound African fetus. James was standing at her side, shaking his head and muttering over and over, "This is a catastrophe, just a catastrophe."

As we struggled to reestablish functional IV access, the story unfolded. She had arrived about four hours earlier in troubled labor. James had been notified but was given such incomplete and poor information that he'd sent the staff back to the hospital to learn more. They returned with more information alright—four hours later! In the interim, IV oxytocin had been initiated, but unfortunately this had only worsened her condition, a bleeding, ruptured uterus. She had been bleeding to death the whole time, more vigorously since the oxytocin had been started. Now, with perfectly deadly timing, the IV had quit working just when we needed to rapidly infuse fluids her heart needed to pump around the half-dozen red blood cells I hoped she had left.

Through the haze that was clearing from my mind, I thought that if we ended up having to code this woman, there was no more epinephrine in the hospital (thanks to yours truly). This was shortly followed by the realization that the woman was no longer breathing. A feeling of dread came over me; we still hadn't gotten another IV, and that if we didn't act fast, we were going to lose two patients, not one. James quickly started running the code, and chest compressions were started while I got an IV in her external jugular. We considered putting in a breathing tube, but with no oxygen to administer, I saw no advantage in that over a simple jaw lift to keep the tongue forward and maintain a patent airway in this tiny woman.

We got the vital signs monitor from the OR and attached it to the patient. The pulse oximeter on her finger was indeed reading in sync with the chest compressions, indicating that the compressions were pumping blood to her extremities. We couldn't obtain a measurement of blood pressure, and there were no EKG patches to check her heart rhythm. And with no epinephrine to administer, this was not exactly going to be a textbook example of CPR. Meanwhile, the husband, standing just outside the room's screened and draped window in the cover of darkness, could be heard asking bystanders in Arabic why we couldn't just cut the baby out if there were problems.

After a few minutes, I got the distinct feeling we were attempting to resuscitate the dead. On one or two occasions I remember thinking, "We should stop this, it's just futile." But I bit my tongue. I could see James was dedicated to trying his best to pull this woman from the jaws of death, and I just couldn't bring myself to oppose the effort.

We took her to the OR, transfused multiple units of blood, tied off her uterine arteries, and poured in two packets of Celox™ to stop the bleeding. In the whirl of activity, James remembered that there were some epidural kit trays in the next room on the storage shelves, where we could find 1-mg vials of epinephrine to compliment the atropine I had already given the patient once we moved her to the OR. We shocked her with a defibrillator but could see little activity on the EKG. Nothing helped. Two and a half long hours after starting the code, we stopped out of futility and discouragement.

As it turned out, the child inside her broken body was hydrocephalic and had spina bifida. The large, alien-like head never would have been able to pass through her pelvis, nor would it have lived long, if at all, after being born. We carefully cleaned off her blood-stained body, covering it with the long, gold-threaded, silk cloth covering she had worn when she arrived. It was time to give her back to her husband. I cringed while wondering if he would fully understand what had just happened to his young wife.

He met us at the door, in the early morning light, as we lowered her cold body onto the ground. I watched as the realization of what he didn't want to know swept across his darkly creased countenance, quickly replacing whatever measure of hope and joy that I can only imagine a husband and father has at the birth of his first child. For once, I was glad I couldn't speak Arabic. With the Arabic he knew, as best he could, James told the story of what had happened to the man's wife and son. As James spoke, the man slowly sank to his knees, uncovering his wife's face to see the truth for himself, cradling her face in both of his hands as he looked closely at her expressionless face. The other men quickly came to his side, responding to his call for water, as he washed her face and closed her eyelids with his fingers. He then covered her face again with the same veil I imagine she had moved aside to kiss him for the first time after they married. He paused for a moment in painful silence as dawn began to break across the gray sky above us. He straightened himself up, and began to softly, yet bitterly, weep and mournfully chant, rocking back and forth while kneeling next to her, surrounded and consoled by his Muslim brothers.

As James and I walked away, he asked me if I knew what the man was saying, over and over again. James translated. "He's saying, 'There is no God but Allah. Allah be praised.'

It stopped me cold. I paused and looked back at the scene of the story we had just experienced. There was no angry yelling or fist waving. No threats of lawsuit or accusations of neglect. Simply genuine expressions of loss and sadness. Nothing more.

"How many Christians do you think would respond like that if this happened to them?" James wondered aloud. We both knew the answer, although we didn't say it out loud. Why embarrass ourselves?

ॐ

Allah!
There is no god but He
The Living, the Self-Subsisting, Eternal.
It is He Who sent down to thee (step by step), in truth, the Book,
Confirming what went before it; and He sent down the Torah (of Moses)
And the Gospel (of Jesus) before this, as a guide to mankind…
He it is Who shapes you in the wombs as He pleases.
There is no god but He…
The Qur'an 3:2-4, 6

White Man Can't Jump

The Toyota van that was rumored to be our transportation back to the capital was not functioning well. For that reason we'd had to hire a truck to take us from Kelo to Bere when we'd first arrived. Weeks later, after recharging the battery and having some work done on the distributor, it still had not been upgraded from its "unreliable" designation. The problem likely originated during a drive through a flooded road during the rainy season. Given the muddy residue in the space where the battery was bolted down, we suspected that water had gotten into one of the hoses of the engine. Although there were just a few days before the truck was needed to return Suzanne and I to civilization, I was strangely calm and nonchalant about the whole prospect of being stranded in the Chadian desert. I'd been around long enough in these places and situations not to worry too much about it.

Next to the covered car port where the van was parked was a small concrete slab and a basketball goal post, complete with backboard and net (surprisingly). One afternoon, while milling around next to this failing experiment in rural transportation and wondering if I should have booked an open-ended return ticket, I let myself get sucked into a game of two-on-two basketball. I really didn't want to play. I mean, I hadn't actually dribbled a basketball in this millennium. I was short. My shoes had been stolen. The rubber sandals I had gotten at market were two sizes too big. I hadn't had surgery yet to remove the cyst on top of my left foot. But I was going to be on James's team—he was about 6' 3", and I figured that we'd get beat so quickly my feet wouldn't have time to develop blisters as I ran around trying to pump and fake jump shots on the rough surface. So we began our quest to be the first team to score ten baskets.

Located on the hospital grounds, the court was on the inside of the chain link fence. However, the main road was only about twenty feet away, and as four white guys began playing basketball, a small crowd pressed their faces into the fence to watch. It was like they'd never seen a game of basketball or something. Some of them even climbed part way up to see over the people standing in front of them. I wasn't sure if they wanted to see a game of basketball or if they just thought it was just a chance to see white people without shirts get hurt. James had told me that the common belief among Africans is that white skin is really flimsy, that it doesn't hold up well, cuts easy during surgery, and doesn't heal well. That kind of stuff. With the hair that's all stringy, straight, and flops all around, white skin couldn't be all that durable. You know how it goes.

Without going into deep detail on the play by play, let me just tell you that this white man may not jump, but he's got a killer sky hook. When I was in grade school, I never could manage to shoot over the reach of anybody in my class. But one afternoon while watching ESPN, I had seen Wilt Chamberlain do this slow, easy-looking sky hook shot over anybody and everybody and thought I'd start trying the same maneuver. I got to the point where I could make the shot if I was right at the three-point line. Any closer and I'd usually shoot too high or hard, but any farther away and I wouldn't come close enough. Unfortunately for James and me, that had been nearly a quarter century ago, and there was no such thing as a three-point line anywhere in this country, let alone this court.

Well, we came right down to the wire. James and I led by only one point, and we needed one more to win. Somehow, the shorter half of the team got possession of the ball, and I dribbled to the right side of the court, around to where I imagined the three-point range was. Then I took one step back away from the goal and pushed upward into the air using the beginnings of a large blister under the large toe of my left foot. As my body rocketed a good two to three inches heavenward, my right leg instinctively bent at the hip and knee, while my right arm and hand (entirely incapable of palming or even gripping the ball very well) performed a scooping, yet graceful, arch in space as I lobbed the ball towards what would be the game-winning goal. Time slowed. I could hear the ball pass through the air, propelled by the anticipation of at least a dozen small African children, each letting out little gasps from behind the fence as they squirmed to see whether or not this inconceivable shot was going … going … going … Yesssss! It went in! Nothing but net! Oh, glorious victory! The sweetness! The triumph of the underdog and of the short!

At least, that's how I remember it. Perhaps it looked more like Daniel in *The Karate Kid* trying out Mr. Miyagi's "Crane" technique for the first time. I don't know, but it's like the master said, "If do right, no can defense." Ask James; he saw it all. I don't know if he believed what he saw, but he did see it. And he didn't complain about winning either.

Speaking of keeping your eye on the ball, a man came in for surgery shortly thereafter. He had a collection of fluid around his testicle that was giving him a lot of trouble. I did a spinal, and James cut out the fluid collection, along with the large, swollen, slick, and rather oblong testicle. As we moved the patient over onto the gurney so he could be rolled out to the hospital ward, I heard a thud followed by a kind of splat, bounce, bounce sound. Out of the corner of my eye I could see Abel, the OR scrub tech, briefly scamper around groping at something on the floor. It quickly became clear that Abel had … well, how shall I say this? Quite literally, he had dropped the ball. I suppose it was understandable. The size, shape, and slick surface combined to make it very difficult to regain control of the ball after initially losing possession. He finally got a grip and, holding it with both hands, slowly stood upright under the curious gaze of all us in the OR, including the patient, who'd been awake the whole time due to the spinal anesthesia. "Abel, my man," I said, as I slapped him on the back, "you need to keep your eye on the ball."

Things you don't want to hear in the mission field:
"If you lift up the passenger's seat, unbolt the engine cover, and hold down the flap mechanism of the carburetor, the engine starts up much more easily. Three cranks instead of twenty. You'll probably want to leave the cover off as you travel to N'Djamena so you can manipulate it as you drive. Otherwise it may stall and who knows if you'll ever get it started again. It does make the inside of the van quite hot though."

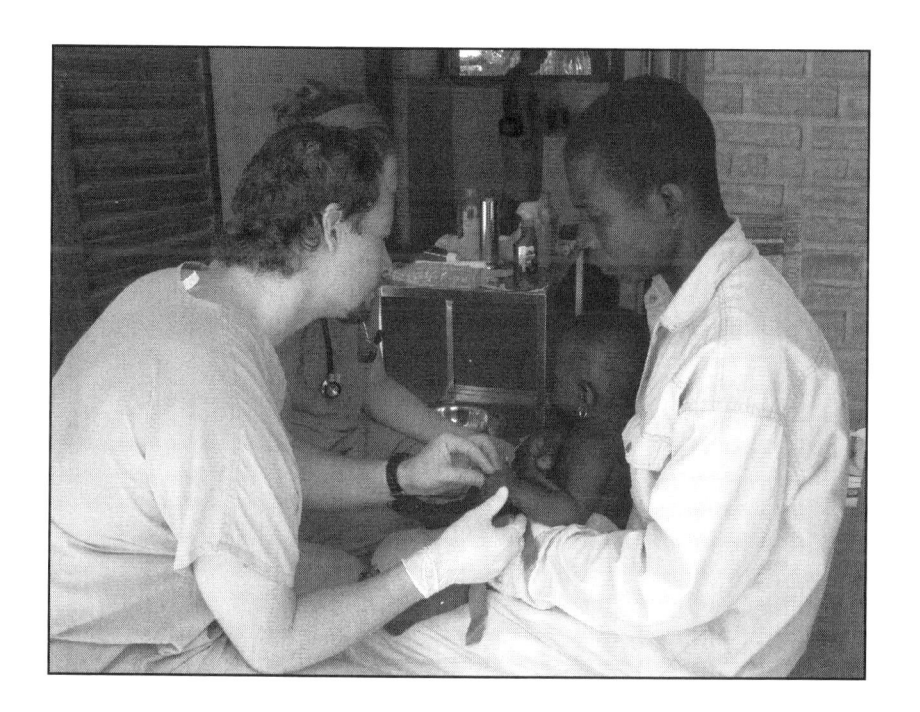

Just Another Day in Paradise

I'm not sure if it was because they actually trusted me and had faith in my doctoring abilities, or if they were simply overwhelmed by the work, but I was asked to see medical patients in the ER. I had actually already helped out for a little while on a couple of days that month. There was usually a steady stream of patients arriving from shortly after sunrise until around sundown, sometimes later. I agreed, even though my French was not nearly what I needed to communicate well with the nurses and patients. But there was at least one person there who could help interpret for me when necessary. With that main concern addressed, I got my pen and stethoscope and marched over to the ER, attempting to remember my past patchwork of tropical medicine experience.

The ER, or urgent care center, was an open room about twenty-five feet wide and fifty feet long. The building didn't really have a door; you simply entered from the outside by drawing aside a colorful green patterned sheet suspended by a string over the inside of the doorway. Immediately inside, there was a desk to the left, where the nurse sat. To the right were a chair and a scale where doctors conducted interviews and weighed patients (mostly, to calculate proper drug doses). From there, patients were assigned one of five exam tables, which extended beyond the nurse's desk along the left wall. There were no curtains around the tables in the room. Regardless of age or sex, patients were examined, often largely disrobed, in a perfunctory manner without regard to their surroundings. One advantage to this arrangement was that if someone had trouble understanding a particular language, the nurse could just call out to anyone in the room in search of a translator.

One of my first cases was an old man who had difficulty urinating. He wore an old, dark brown trench coat, which at this point in my stay no longer surprised me, despite the triple-digit temperatures. I learned through an interpreter that he had the typical history of benign prostatic hypertrophy. I then tried for what seemed like the next ten minutes to explain to him how he was supposed to position himself during a prostate exam. He seemed totally bewildered, as was I, come to think of it. I mean, it wasn't brain surgery. It was a rectal exam. How hard could it be? Even an anesthesiologist could do one. Anyway, after I performed the exam and felt what I believed to be a very large, smooth, slightly tender prostate, I relieved him of my professional digital services and rendered my opinion via the interpreter. We scheduled him for surgery to remove his prostate the following day.

The next patient was a woman who'd had a large kidney tumor removed about three months ago by a visiting surgeon at Bere. Currently, she was having a very hard time using her right arm. I could see that her muscles had begun to shrink, compared to those of the left arm. The strength on the right side was obviously weak. I put my hand on her shoulder as I examined her and had the distinct sense that she was a little too bony, even for an African. I took a closer look. Her shoulder blade was sticking out more than you'd expect. I compared it to the other side. "Well, well," I thought. "Haven't seen one of these for a while." It was a winging scapula, a condition in which the shoulder blade sticks out of the back, looking like a little angel's wing. Usually, the cause is related to dysfunction of a specific nerve that runs up the side of the chest to the muscles that pull on the underside of that bone, holding it flat against the back. I suspected that she'd had some prolonged nerve compression or bruising during her last surgery, but had no way of confirming this, since the surgeon who had performed the operation was long gone. When I told James about the case, he told me he had actually been there and assisted during the operation.

"So, was this lady's right arm stretched out above her head like this maybe?" I asked, as I made a motion showing how I imagined her lying for the six-hour case.

"Yeah. It was something like that."

"Well, that was probably what did it to her," I said. "It's a known complication of positioning. There's really nothing to do for her; even if there were neurologists in this country, they could offer no treatment. In about three to six months, much of the function should return after an injury of this nature, but there's no guarantee. We'll just have to wait and see." The interpreter relayed the information to her for us, and I went on to see the next patient.

Sarah saw me coming as I approached the nurse's desk to ask for my next assignment, and she unceremoniously announced that I needed to drain the large collection of abdominal fluid from the HIV-positive lady waiting for me on the third exam table. "Great," I thought. "a problem I've already done once before. Maybe I'll get good at this outpatient stuff after all!"

I went to the OR to pick up some Betadine, a pair of gloves, a big 14-gauge needle, and a basin in which to drain the fluid. When I came over to the patient, she just lay down and lifted the side of her blouse without a word, exposing her left side and belly.

"She's had it done before," Sarah called out to me from across the room, without looking up from her work. "She knows what you'll do."

It felt a little odd, as it always did, to doing something to someone without talking with her about all the details, risks, benefits etc. But I was acclimating as best I could. I looked at her, knowing she knew no English, and said, "Ma'am, this is going to hurt you more than it is going to hurt me." And with that, I pushed a large needle into her side, slid off the catheter after pulling the needle back out, and had her son hold the basin to catch the fluid that came streaming out of her side. She didn't even flinch, just smiled a bit, knowing she'd be able to breath, eat and sleep easier after she was relieved of this watery bulge that had repeatedly plagued her. I watched the flow of clear yellow fluid long enough to convince myself that her bowels weren't going to interrupt this treatment by plugging up the end of the catheter, then walked back to the OR for one last case for the day. It turned out to be a real doozy.

This patient had a very large tumor growing on his kidney. Our job was to open him up, check for visible evidence of widespread metastasis, and then, based on our findings, either close up an inoperable case of cancer or perform a wide resection. My part of the deal, as usual, was to make James's job as easy as possible, while at the same time keeping the patient's physiology within acceptable limits and the man himself physically comfortable. Or at the very least, entirely forgetful, thanks to a vial or two of valium.

Once again, the position of the surgical site made an anesthetic of ketamine alone a poor choice. James had to work deep down in the patient's side, fighting against the action of a moving diaphragm and reflexive resistance of unrelaxed abdominal muscles. Further complicating matters was the overall dearth of useable long surgical instruments to reach down into the dark cavity, all the while using less than the brightest of overhead lights (running on that 1930s generator that was at least fifty years past its useful lifespan). On the other hand, a spinal normally would not extend that high in the abdomen for very long. And even if it did, the anesthetic level likely would begin to recede as the spinal wore off, probably just when James most needed it to be working best. Furthermore, with that much pressure on the diaphragm and lower portion of his lungs, I was concerned that the patient would not get enough oxygen from room air alone. Of course, we could turn on the oxygen concentrator to extract the nitrogen from the room air, leaving only compressed oxygen to be delivered to the patient via mask. But that was assuming that the generator was running properly. And if all that weren't enough, experience had shown that turning on the concentrator put enough drain on its specific electrical circuit that something else in the OR would have to be turned off in order for enough current to remain to run the concentrator. In order to have oxygen, we would have to make a decision to forego, at least temporarily, the use of something we really did not want to go without ... like the lights, vital sign monitors, or electrocautery. What was I going to do?

We made a plan. I would dose up another high spinal with the longest acting, unexpired, local anesthetic we had on hand. And this time I would be more prepared for dangerously low blood pressure after pilfering a couple of ampoules of epinephrine from the epidural kits James had found in storage during the flurry of our last resuscitative fiasco. If the cancer had already spread, there would be nothing more for us to do, and the surgery would be over in about fifteen minutes. If it was still sufficiently isolated, we would cut it out and go for a surgical cure. James agreed to try to use an old, but powerfully bright headlight that had proven a bit too cumbersome to wear the first and last time he had tried to use it. This would help him see deep down inside the surgical cavity, where the more dimly lit, antiquated, overhead lights tended to be essentially useless. This donated headlight (made in the United States) was an exciting exception to the Junk for Jesus rule, but it used 110 volts, which allowed me to run it from a different electrical circuit than we had to use for the other 220-volt equipment, like the oxygen concentrator and overhead lights. This would open up the possibility of shutting the overheads off altogether, liberating enough excess current to run the oxygen concentrator on the 220-volt system.

To our good fortune, I also had found a precious few extra-long surgical instruments in a forty-foot shipping container next to the guest house, and these had been sterilized just in time to be used for this case. James was greatly relieved to have these available for this particular procedure. This is not to say that they were exceptions to the Junk for Jesus rule. They weren't. But they were all we had, and they were usable even though I had to sharpen the scissors with the knife sharpener I'd had the foresight to bring with me.

I used the entire 20 mg contained in the bupivicaine spinal ampoule, along with 200 micrograms of epinephrine, in an attempt to maximize the duration of action. Then I tipped the head of the bed down so that gravity would pull the drug downward, extending the numb, paralyzed area in which James would have to work. After leaving it there for about ten minutes, I leveled the table in an attempt to prevent an excessive block from developing and causing low blood pressure or a slow heart rate (or worse, a cardiac arrest). My backup plan if the spinal started to wear off was to switch to ketamine for the remaining duration of the case. Hopefully, this would be after the more challenging exposure and resection of the tumor was complete. From there it would be downhill for James to finish up.

James and Abel got scrubbed, gowned, and gloved and then stepped under the overhead lights which, from personal experience, I can tell you generate much more heat than light. And this was on just another day in paradise, where the temperature was already about 105 degrees Fahrenheit. Actually, it could have been worse. Sometimes it gets up to 130 degrees Fahrenheit, so it was hard to complain. Well, no. I take it back. Actually, it would have been quite easy to complain. I just didn't do it out loud. After all, I didn't want James to think I was a weenie.

Things got underway without any problems. James was working way up next to the diaphragm with no trouble, and the patient didn't seem to be feeling any pain at all. And even if he were, thanks to 20 mg of valium he wouldn't remember it anyway. And to be honest, with that much valium in a skinny, older man, he probably wasn't going to remember much of anything until after next weekend.

After a thorough inspection, James concluded that the tumor was well contained and resectable, without evidence of metastatic disease. The next step would be to carefully dissect its borders, isolate its blood supply, tie it off before the patient bled too much, cut out that big, bad boy, and sew the patient shut again. Maybe this wasn't going to be so bad after all, I thought.

You'd think I'd learn my lesson to not think or say stuff like that, but no! Shortly thereafter I was battling some of the lowest blood pressure I had seen on the continent. I slapped the guy around a bit on his face to see if he was at all responsive, not caring for the moment that he was probably chief, ruler, magistrate, and judge over just about all you could see out the window all the way to the horizon and beyond. I got nothing, no response at all. I briefly considered that his lack of response could have been related solely to the valium, but I knew at the beginning of the case he would at least look toward your voice if you yelled. I told James what was going on with the blood pressure, without details about the loss of consciousness, which I selfishly kept to myself. "That can't be right!" James replied. "Check it again. After all, the pulse oximeter wouldn't be picking up a pulse if it was less than sixty or so, right?"

Technically, that was true, but still the blood pressure really was in the fifties the second time I measured it. So rather than debating the finer points of cardiovascular physiology, I simply reached for a syringe of epinephrine and squirted enough into his vein to make me feel better. And I did feel better, especially after his blood pressure reached normal limits again.

Bliss rarely lasts in the OR though. One of the things that shatters the serenity is the sound of a sterile surgical instrument hitting the floor after someone loses control of it. In many institutions in America this event generally is followed by a cascade of verbal blue streaks, and an abrupt period of silence during which people wait for any secondary aftershocks to emanate from the surgeon's mouth. In truth, these incidents are usually very minor problems in the United States because you can either get another matching sterile instrument from off the rack or do a quick "flash" on the dropped one, a process which completes the sterilization of an object in about five minutes instead of the usual forty-five. But we weren't in the United States. We were in Chad. And there was no five-second rule. We were going to have to make due because there were no spares. And even if we did fire up the sterilizer, by the time we had built the charcoal fire, got it hot enough to complete the sterilization process, then let the thing cool down enough to touch it, the spinal would have worn off hours ago.

The only thing worse than hearing something long, important, and metallic strike the hot, concrete floor of a mission hospital eight hours away from the capital city is hearing a second something that's long, important, and metallic strike that hot, concrete floor. (And the city is eight hours away only if you have enough cash to bribe your way through each of the police checkpoints, both going and coming!) From my perspective, I can say James did an admirable job of keeping his religion after hearing the loud clanging noise of his super-sized needle driver hit the floor. There were the obligatory, firm, vociferous admonitions in French to his nearly deaf assistant, who couldn't read lips behind a surgical mask anyway, about how impossible it would be to replace those tools in this critical moment. But overall, he kept his cool pretty well in that concrete oven we called the OR.

Now it was my turn. After an hour and a half of pushing on his diaphragm, the patient's lower lungs were not expanding well enough to take in the maximum amount of oxygen from the air. This, combined with the fact that the spinal was beginning to recede—which allowed his abdomen to tighten up more and squeeze the lower chest—was leaving him smaller breaths with which to load the circulating blood with oxygen as it passed through the lungs. I began juggling electrical loads so I could power up the oxygen concentrator. I debated with James about which things I could turn off, when, and for how long, but in the end we decided to go without the overhead lights. They took the most power, and besides, the headlamp he was using was working well. Trying to get the patient's oxygen level back up to normal without blowing any fuses, I used my third and fourth arms to administer an extra dose of ketamine into his IV bottle that would drip in over time as an infusion. After another hour or so of clamping and whirlwind sewing on James's part, and go-go-gadget arm and leg deploying on my part, we actually managed to finish the case and sighed together in weary relief.

No sooner had we left that patient in the ward to recover, then there was a patient who came to the ER with a dislocated jaw. James asked me and Jacques, the new medical school graduate visiting Bere from Ghana, to check it out and see what needed to be done. When I got there, I looked around at the faces of the people who were waiting. It was easy to spot her, sitting alone with her mouth agape, wearing a forlorn expression. I glanced around the room looking for Sarah, who was always my first choice for interpretive services. "How did she do it?" I asked.

"She said it happened while she was yawning."

"Oh, really?" I mused aloud sarcastically. I felt around her jaw bone, back where the joint hinges below the ear. I looked at her in the eyes, but she wouldn't look back at me. "You don't say." I didn't buy it for a second. Most yawns aren't strong enough to break a paper bag, let alone dislocate a jaw bone on both sides. The way I saw it, someone had hit her, hard. And probably not all that recently, as I could see little remaining evidence of bruising or swelling. Whoever it was, that someone was not with her. I suspected the husband. I asked Sarah if she could try to get a little more information about what was going on.

After a few exchanges, Sarah said, "She says she was also gored by a bull. In the mouth."

"Oh yeah? When was that?"

Sarah asked, and then told me, "A few weeks, maybe two or three. She says she doesn't know." I shook my head. Classic, just classic.

"You know, if I got gored in the mouth by a bull, I think I would remember it." This lady easily could have been mistaken for the typical knife-and-gun club member that rolls into big city emergency rooms in America on a Friday or Saturday night. I imagined the story she might tell: "Honest, Doc, I was just minding my own business in the rice fields when this big bull...."

"Okay, okay. Fine. It doesn't matter how it happened. What matters is, what are we going to do about it?" I thought about it for a second and said, "I suppose we could just dose her up with some ketamine and relocate the joint." And I meant it, I really meant it. See, I was supposing because I had never actually done it before.

I walked over to James's house to tell him the story and what I planned to do, all the while trying to remember the details of the only other jaw dislocation I had ever even heard of. When I told him about this lady's story, he was as doubtful as I was. After he took his turn interrogating her, we looked inside her mouth with the light I had brought from the guest house. Sure enough, there was a small, dark discoloration in the roof of her mouth marking the very center of her hard pallet. "Humph. Whaddya know?" I thought out loud. I was still skeptical, having never seen bulls around there with horns that small. "You think a bull's horn did that?" I asked James, as we both squinted into her halfway open mouth, her jaw swung awkwardly out to the left side.

We didn't really know what to think. But I'm not sure either of us really thought it mattered anymore. So, Jacques and I went off to the OR and after an intramuscular injection of ketamine and three attempts to remedy the dislocation, we succeeded in returning the woman's face to its normal appearance. Much later I remembered that the only other case of dislocated jaw I knew about was on an episode of *Trauma: Life in the E.R*, broadcast several years before I went to medical school. If I remember, a graduate student had been brought in by his miffed roommate. The student had been pulling an all-nighter studying in the library when his jaw popped out of socket after one big, long, *major* yawn. It was locked wide open, leaving him nearly unable to talk. I couldn't remember if the ER resident believed the story he was told anymore readily than I had. But what I did remember was that they had struggled a lot longer than Jacques and I did to get the jaw back into place. And I don't remember him using any sedation or pain killers either. Even in deepest, darkest Africa, we give people sedation and pain killers to relocate their jaw. Americans, they can be so barbaric!

༄༅༄

Things you don't want to hear in the mission field:
"No, I'm not kidding. We're about out of charcoal."

Two Is One, and One Is None

I remember seeing him the first day I arrived at the hospital. He was in the middle bed, on the right-hand side of the pediatric ward, surrounded by a large number of family members. He had led the average life of an African boy. But in the past several months he had started to bleed, spontaneously, and for no apparent reason. James had struggled for a long time to help him, but a conclusive diagnosis had been elusive, and no form of empiric treatments had afforded any improvement in his condition. The rise in his hemoglobin level following frequent whole blood transfusions from family members had proven to be surprisingly short lived. His body would either consume or sequester all of it somehow, or bleed it out his rectum.

At this point in time, his family was unwilling to give any more blood. Initially, I was shocked at their resistance. But, after considering the futility they had seen follow their prolonged efforts, I sympathized with them. After all, what good had it done? He simply was not getting any better.

The only lead we had was that James had been able to feel polyps during a rectal exam he had performed after the boy's nose bleeds migrated south and manifested as gastrointestinal bleeding. The only thing left on the differential diagnosis was familial polyposis, a genetic disorder where bleeding typically occurs from thousands of polyps lining the colon. Unfortunately, there was no colonoscope that James could use to confirm or rule out that diagnosis. That is, not until I found two inside the shipping container. James was especially excited to have these additions to his armamentarium of tools in this remote, primitive setting. After all, two is one, and one is none.

I immediately went to work trying to find a light source for the fiber-optic cables that would allow us to see up inside this boy past the place where the Saharan sun doesn't shine. There had been one near the two scopes in storage, but it didn't look to be in very good condition. Call me a pessimist, but I was afraid it wouldn't work. Furthermore, I knew that even if it did work, like most of the Junk for Jesus that is sent to a continent supplied exclusively with 220 volts, it would probably require 110 volts. And I had no idea if we had enough current to make it work. I just hoped that it would not have to be used simultaneously with any other of our 110-volt equipment. I walked back to the storage container and unlocked the door as I mulled all this over in my mind. I swung open the huge door to the forty-foot-long dark chamber of medical junk, hoping that for once I could find a small treasure chest in the form of a functional light source. I walked past the IV fluid reserves stacked to the ceiling and waded knee deep through the crumbling, cobweb-covered cardboard boxes to the place I had found the scopes, looking for the light source I remembered seeing. Ah-ha! There it was. I yanked it from its position, wedged between other objects leaning and falling on top of it. I supported its heavy weight against my stomach as I tried to turn it around in my hands, like a father hoping to find out the gender of his newborn.

Dang. It was the wrong kind of plug. When I got back to the States, I planned to have a word with the stupid storks that kept delivering those babies over here.

I trudged back over to the operating room, wired with the limiting supply of 110 volts. After the generator was fired up, I plugged the thing in and double-checked the current requirement on the back before flipping the switch on the front. Egad! The thing nearly blinded me as it lit up brighter than a Manhattan Project gone awry. I flailed my arms and hands around in front of my face as I searched for the switch again, desperately seeking to shade my vision and glimpse the front panel just long enough to feel for the right place to shut off the artificial light.

After my retinas had sufficiently recovered from this pleasantly surprising blast of illumination, I was able to open the cases of the two colonoscopes and determine if they could indeed be connected to the light source. It quickly became apparent that one of the colonoscopes had no functional controls. There was no way to move the camera left, right, up or down. You could see through it though, so I figured all was not lost. At least, that's what I thought until I figured out the light source had a different connection than that needed for the scope. Okay, then! One down, one to go. Two is one, and one is none, right?

The other scope had been manufactured by the same company whose name was on the light source, so it connected easily, although a bit loosely. The light lit up the end of the fiberscope nicely. I looked through the lens and was able to see a fish-eyed image of the OR bed in front of me. It was upside down, so I flipped the camera handle 180 degrees in my hand and started fiddling with the rotational controls. It took me about a minute to figure out that about half of the entire 360 degrees of rotation were not working. As I thought about whether or not it would be good enough for James to get any use out of it, my eyes fell on a piece of paper inside the colonoscope case. It was a single page with a letter head from the manufacturer. It was short and to the point. *The scope was out of warranty and being returned to the client per their own request after having declined to pay for the required extensive repairs.*

And so, truly, two had been one, and one had proven to be none. Thanks to all those fine people at Christian hospitals back in America, we were no better off than before they supplied us with these valuable donations (i.e., tax write-offs). Those sons of motherless goats! God have mercy on their sanctimonious souls. They'll need it if his name turns out to be Allah.

I put the colonoscope back in its case. Evidently the locals in Chad would enjoy a respite before they too had to learn to ride "the little black pony" at a white man's hospital. Until then, I supposed I could barter the thing away at market. After all, it came in such a nice plastic suitcase, complete with locking latches. In keeping with the African tradition, these locks would be supplied without keys. Perhaps if I could convince an Arab trader at the market that with this magical device he could see around corners, he would give me a nice bar of soap, half a kilo of tea, and a cup of sugar. You laugh, but I bet he would.

Peek and Shriek

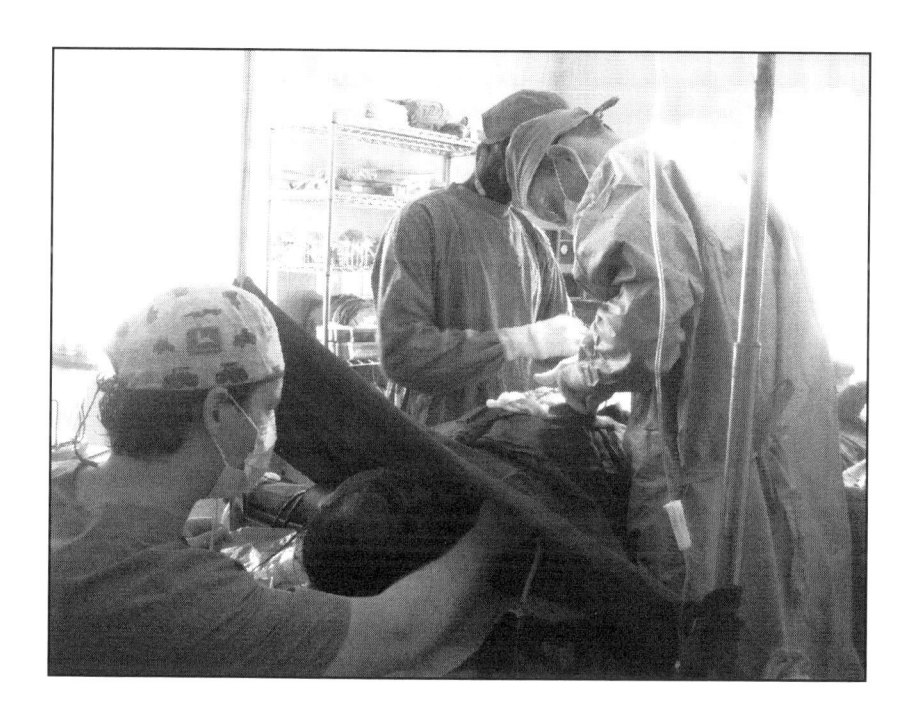

"I'd like to operate on that little boy while I still have you here. It's going to be complicated." James had debated a long time about if, when, and how he would operate on the child who'd been bleeding due to polyps. He had considered leaving the case alone for fear of having to deal with some kind of rectal reconstruction, which would have taken him out of his surgical experience and comfort zone. Greg Shank could have handled it. He was the surgeon who (along with his wife, who had graduated with James and me) ran a small mission hospital west of us, over the border in Cameroon. But the bush pilot we'd been waiting for had not yet arrived at the hospital, and we needed his services to facilitate transportation of the patient or, more likely, the surgeon.

James continued, "The good news is, I learned last night as I studied for this case that in the setting of familial polyposis, I don't have to do anything with the rectum. So it should be a straight forward resection, much easier than I thought." I'm not sure why the phrases, "good news," and "much easier," failed to trigger some kind of instinctive or reflexive resistance in the part of my brain that accumulated experience in mission anesthesia and surgical care. But they didn't. All I knew was that this was probably going to be the youngest patient I'd ever done a spinal on; if anyone was likely to bleed to death in front of me, it was going to be him. Using ketamine would make an intestinal operation through an abdominal incision unnecessarily challenging for James. Spinal anesthesia was the only other option, since there were no usable anesthesia machine or gases available. As for blood transfusion, the only questions were from whom would it come and, of equal importance, if it would come.

The case got started the day before I left Chad, but only after we had obtained as much blood and clotting factors as we could. There was only one unit of the blood donated previously by compatible family members left over in the fridge, and it had begun to leak badly out of its plastic bag after it had been hung outside to warm in the sun. It was nothing a large clamp, strategically positioned, couldn't stop. Fortunately for all of us, three other units had been given by volunteers. These were whole blood, containing platelets and clotting factors that would be critical for the boy to have. Several units of fresh frozen plasma, with clotting factors, were thawing also.

After starting as big an IV as I could fit in his vein, I performed a spinal. The rest of the team placed a Foley catheter to drain his bladder, and prepped and draped his abdomen. As always, we stopped to pray. Then we were ready to begin.

To cut a long story short, this kid bled badly from the get-go. It wouldn't have been so bad if I'd had more time to raise his hemoglobin level from where it was at 2.4 gm/dl (the lowest I have ever seen, approximately 10 points below normal). But after hosing in everything I had, the bleeding nearly stopped and his hemoglobin was almost 9. This was good. But James found no polyps. This was bad. It erased all our ideas about what we *thought* we were dealing with. He scrubbed out and did another rectal exam, which was much easier to perform under spinal anesthesia. He found a large rectal tumor, making this the third child I had seen in a month with advanced cancer. We closed him back up. There was no more to be done.

ෆන්

Things you don't want to hear in the mission field:
"You know, the medical officers on night shift use that sink to pee in."

Yes, I Am a Doctor, and This Is My Arabian Port-o-Potty

It was time to pack our things to leave. Suzanne and I went through all our stuff to be sure we weren't missing anything (other than my shoes) and that all our travel documents were in order to minimize the problems we fully expected to meet at the Chadian immigration desk. We had our letters of invitation, passports, and Suzanne's immunization records. As mentioned earlier, I had forgotten my yellow fever documentation in the United States. When Suzanne and I had arrived, I had been lucky because the authorities never asked to see our records. We were the very last ones in line, it was so late at night, and our French was so pitifully bad, they must have just wanted to get rid of us. They eventually shook their heads wearily and waved us through and into their country.

Fortunately for me, immunizations are not reviewed when you leave, so in that respect I felt that I was in the clear. But I wondered if they might use that as a trick to get me to pay something. As I thought about this possibility and looked over Suzanne's documents, I let my eyes wander down the list of numerous immunizations she had gotten before coming. I smiled as I remembered having to actually talk her into getting the meningitis vaccine. "Do you really think I'll need it?" she had asked. After a thirty-second description of what it would be like to actually have meningitis, she agreed to get it, along with *all* the other recommended vaccines.

My brief flashback was interrupted by the last, handwritten line on her immunization and yellow fever record. It confused me. I had never heard of this immunization before. I wasn't even sure I could read it. I turned to Suzanne, who was packing her bag next to me, and asked her, "What's this here?" I pointed to the line as she turned towards me. "What in the world is 'tee breading?" It sounded like something the English would do while drinking Earl Gray.

"Tee breading?" she repeated with a confused but inquisitive expression on her face as she peered over my shoulder. "What are you talking about?"

"This. Right here. Your last immunization. It says you had a tee breading." Her face lost all expression for a moment, and then she turned to me and calmly, slowly but with emphasis said, "It says I had a TB reading, *Doctor*."

"Oh yeah. ... yeah, it does, doesn't it." I mumbled as I nodded, and then added, "I am a doctor." She turned back to her packing and busted up laughing, "I don't know, Cuz, you worry me!" She then called to everyone within earshot and motioned for them to look at the "immunization" record so that they too could enjoy my humiliation. I like to think that they really weren't laughing at me; they were just laughing near me.

We left early the next morning, after getting up at four a.m. to pack the marginally functional minivan that allegedly was going to transport us eight hours to N'Djamena. Suzanne and I had elected to wear the local garb for the trip home, mostly because it would be the last chance we got to wear that style for a very long time. She had a violet head scarf with gold trim to go with a brown dress. I had a light purple turban to go with the long, sky blue Arab style robe-like shirt. I had gotten it yesterday, just in the nick of time before leaving the country. This was over a week later than had been promised by the "tailor" who had measured me and promised to put a cool embroidered pattern on the front (which he couldn't because, as it turned out, he didn't know how!). If I was going to get to wear this made-to-fit outfit at all, it was going to be on our last day in Bere.

"Hey, nice suit Omar!" James walked over towards me through the just-breaking twilight. "Man, you look soooo Arab. You fit right in here! Sure you don't want to stay?" I smiled and wondered how many wives I could get away with. "I could get used to this, actually. This thing is really comfortable. Roomy, too. All I need is a pair of aviator sunglasses, and I could pass as a Libyan!" Some of the others who had gathered to see us off laughed a bit and said they had to agree.

"Now you understand why there are no bathrooms in Chad," James said. "See, everyone is wearing their bathroom already. It's spacious, gives you plenty of room to work in. It's all the privacy you'll ever need. Just squat, do your business, stand up, and walk away!" I paused to look down, staring at myself as this epiphany broke over my consciousness. I stood in awe of this elegant combination of privacy, utility, and flowing, fashionable style I was wearing. Amazing. If necessity is the mother of invention, then this very well could be (to put it in Middle Eastern parlance) the "Mother of All Inventions!"

We turned serious as we realized that it was time for a real good-bye. "Franklin, it was really good having you here," James said. "I hope we get a chance to work together again in the future."

"Me, too," I told him. "I'm glad I came. Don't be surprised if you see me again." We shook hands and I moved on to say my final farewells all around the circle of gathered well-wishers, promising to stay in touch by email. Michel, the French doctor, and his wife were up extra early, and they joined the group who gave us a warm send off. He had never really spoken much English to me, but as he shook my hand, in a very thick accent he assured me, "Your grandfathers fought and died for France. You will always be welcome in our home if you come to Paris." The look in his eye said he was dead serious.

With our driver revving the engine periodically to keep it from stalling, we crammed the last of seventeen people into the minivan before bouncing off for the next two hours down the dirt road from Bere to Kelo. Having been the last sardine placed in this can, I was pressed up against the window side of the vehicle. This meant that when the sun rose at its customary time of 5:15 a.m. to begin its daily trek, blazing a trail across the African sky, I was the first to catch it in the face. I deftly adjusted my new turban to shade myself from the heat and light and couldn't help but feel a bit smug about having learned and applied a bit of Arab wisdom for daily living.

We stopped briefly in Kelo to unload a number of passengers before beginning the next six hours of our journey to N'Djamena. As we journeyed onward, over time, the ever-present irritants of heat and dust were joined by feelings of hunger, weariness, slight motion sickness, and rising internal bladder tension. None of which alone could provoke much discomfort in the seasoned traveler, but the simultaneous combination of all of them proved to be oppressive. As for the hunger, we actually stopped once but I chose not to buy anything with the few francs I had left. This is because I have learned that the roadside food selection available in the typical African town is not close enough to consumable for me to risk my personal health and wellness. I reluctantly stuck it out and got nothing while others munched on newly acquired "snacks." I watched as our driver bought more airtime for his cell phone, and inferred that he had been driving for hours in a vehicle that could quit running at any minute with no means of communication. Personally, I don't even ride without some form of communication.

We drove on. If you went to medical school and did an internship and a residency, you've probably come to the point where being tired, dirty, and sometimes nauseous is really no big deal. It's the full bladder that will get you every time. Unless you're a surgeon; I'm really not sure surgeons have bladders. Anyway, we stopped again shortly after getting out of town and the driver, who spoke no English, attempted to explain the reason for this stop. Regrettably, my French was not good enough to convince him to try that mode of communication either. So using some crude hand gestures, combined with basic sound effects, he made it clear to me that he was about to relieve himself some distance away from the road, of into the bush. Ah, perfect. Now I would get a chance to do some field testing of my new, wearable, Arabian port-o-potty. I could barely contain myself. Literally.

Each passenger made his or her way off into the not so distant horizon to find his or her place of peace among all of God's creatures. Naturally, I can't speak for the others, but without going into all the details, I can say with certainty the Arabs are onto something. You don't live in and dominate the 10/40 window for more than two thousand years without learning a trick or two about living. And now, I, too have learned yet another trick with Arabian clothes. Suffice it to say I grew to love the fashion more and more as the sands of time ebbed and flowed. And I might add, the less time that ebbs before the aforementioned sands cover the places I've paused to squat, the better.

Back in the minivan, the mood was noticeably lighter, in every sense, as we continued driving merrily on toward N'Djamena, dodging pot holes and swerving past goats, cows, and small children. That is, until we hit our first official checkpoint. The officers weren't actually there to enforce any laws. They were there to operate above the law and use their power to obtain any extra cash that eventually had to pass their way. You don't have much of a fighting chance at a roadblock when your team is the only one without fully loaded, well-used, Russian Kalashnikov assault weapons. If you want to make it to the airport at last and not *dead* last, you need to consider doing what they say. And it doesn't help to have all of your papers in order and stamped by the proper government authorities. It doesn't help that the huge sign next to the police officers' booth clearly states that hospital vehicles are exempt. It doesn't help if you've already driven through that same check point several times a month for the past five years. They are still somehow going to come up with some reason to charge someone something for letting you pass through on your way to somewhere. In economics class in high school I learned that, "There is no such thing as a free lunch." Well, John Maynard Keynes's "General Theory of Employment, Interest and Money" simply does not apply in Chad. Whoever says you can't get something for nothing clearly has not traveled through these parts. After we finally arrived at a mutually agreeable fee (i.e., bribe), the local authorities "graciously" allowed us to pass through the roadblock without further haggling or discussion.

We arrived in N'Djamena around two o'clock in the afternoon, navigating the streets without having to stop at either of the capital city's two nearly new stop lights. As we made our way through the various sections of town, residual evidence of an attempted coup in February of that year was especially abundant near the presidential "palace." Bullet holes the size of lemons pockmarked the buildings and walls. Whoever said, "It's a jungle out there" is a lot closer to the mark than the guy who said, "There's no such thing as a free lunch." He's probably the kind of guy who would shoot you in the back, push you off to the side, and then finish eating your lunch for free! Yet, having lived and worked in these kinds of hostile environments, riddled with holes generated with illegal weapons, I still have to say that my thoughts on improving gun-control would begin with encouraging people to use both hands. Especially with the Kalashnikovs, which tend to kick and rise higher as you hold the trigger down in fully automatic mode.

Since we had another eight hours before our flight left, we decided to go to the market, conveniently located near the large central mosque. There, our driver picked up several dozen energy-efficient light bulbs for the hospital, and I got a pair of aviator sunglasses to complete my whole Arabian playboy motif. A month after our first foray into this foreign free-for-all, Suzanne and I returned dressed incognito and armed with more French and Chadian Arabic-language skills. These allowed us to pass the time more leisurely than before, without the constant harassment of every Ahmed, Abdul, and Mohammed asking why I hadn't covered my rebellious woman's head and shoulders or if she were for sale.

It was hot, and I was thirsty. But since this was not my first time in the market, I knew what to do about it. All I had to do was look around for a small boy pushing around a wheel barrow with a cooler in or on it. This cooler likely would contain 250-ml bags of clean drinking water. And, with any luck, the cooler had some ice in it, too. After parking myself on a bench outside what looked like an electrical supply store, all I did was wait. Sure enough. A few minutes later a little guy came by pushing his cooler. It cost about 25 cents to buy a bag each for Suzanne and myself, but only because I remembered the price from last time and didn't even open my mouth to ask how much I had to pay. You have to know the price already and pay exact change or a little more while keeping your hand out in an expectant manner. This indicates that you expect change and implies that you know the price and what you are owed, and a Muslim merchant will not want to be thought of as stealing from you. After securing our liquid assets, I whipped out my trusty Swiss Army knife to slice a hole in each bag, which allowed us to quench our thirst as we unabashedly slurped and sucked out the water.

We spent the rest of the afternoon and evening eating what we called "the last supper," washing the dirt off our travel-weary bodies, and taking a two-hour nap at a guest house before we were dropped off at the airport for the overnight flight that would leave for Paris at 10:50 p.m.

TWA: "Travel with Arabs"

Prior to checking in, we decided to wait in the airport's one restaurant, which was upstairs. There, we could sit on padded chairs, get something to drink, and maybe even use a bathroom with running water. I was surprised to see there was a television set which worked, and we were able to see some news from the rest of the world. Shortly after we sat down, some English-speaking brutes came in and took over the bar section. They didn't need much time to self-medicate their anxious nerves for the long flight ahead of us. I assumed they'd be on our flight since, in this part of the world, if you're at the airport at the same time as someone else you can safely assume that you will leave on the same airplane. This was unfortunate, as their repeated dosing, by all appearances, was having no calming effect on the group whatsoever. My only hope was that they wouldn't be too close to me on the plane. Nonetheless, I would have the luxury of my trusty earplugs and nightshade, and in this I took great comfort. With these hopes and fears mixing in my head, I accompanied Suzanne back downstairs to check in for the flight and pass through security.

Getting out of Chad can be as interesting as getting in. Officials can make up whatever reason they want to make you pay in order to leave. While at the hospital, we were told by others who had come and gone from Chad before us that we could expect to pay an "exit fee" of around U.S. $50 to $100 to get our passports handed back to us after they were stamped for departure. This transaction took place right across from the booth with an officer of the national police. Truth be told, there actually is an exit fee; it just so happens that it's included in the price of your plane ticket and generally written on it, too. Most people don't know this and are so intimidated by the situation that they'll pay anything to go home. That's the case even if they do know that by pointing out the figure printed on the paper ticket they can prove they've already paid the fee. So they often end up paying it again.

Eventually, it was our turn to go through passport control. The officer greeted us in French, and after a month of preconditioning, without thinking we replied in French as well. He looked at our passports, our nationality, our matching last names, and then at us. He seemed a bit surprised by our appearance and asked us where we had been and why we had come to Chad. We did our best to explain in French and English, and also handed him our letters of invitation from the hospital (written in French by James). He looked the letters over without saying anything. Two other officers joined in the "investigation." One of them thanked me for covering my woman's head. They said they liked my suit and said we both seemed to have fit into Chad just fine. Then, the one officer who had all our papers stamped our passports, handed them back to us, and wished us a safe trip. "Wow," I thought to myself. "This suit just paid for itself. I love this thing."

We stepped outside the building to join the other passengers who were waiting to board the plane, which was parked on the tarmac about fifty yards in front of us. Despite this proximity, just like when we arrived, we had to ride in a bus from the steps of the airport to the steps leading up to the plane. We ended up waiting for the bus longer than it would have taken for us to walk.

We crammed onto this little shuttle and braced ourselves for the twenty-second ride. I turned to my left and saw an obviously inebriated white guy staring back at me with googly eyes, his gaze fixed on mine. He clumsily groped for the safety rail with one hand, while trying to handle his luggage with the other. I got the uneasy sense that he was feeling, or imagining, within himself a sense of community with some newly found friend and fellow expatriate … me. Oh, woe is me.

"Hey," he slurred. "Where are you people from?" His British accent was easily discerned above his level of intoxication.

"We're American," I said, motioning with one hand to Suzanne. His face immediately winced into a confused expression, mouth agape.

"Huh?" He paused a bit, looking us up and down.

"Yeah, the United States." I gave him a bit of time to let it sink in. It didn't seem to help, so I added, "You know, the former colonies?" Then I smiled really big.

"Oh," he gasped as he recoiled, half shaking his head with a frown on his face. "That's low, brother." He asked why we were wearing those clothes, but at this point our little ride was over and there was no time to chat with the man. And even if there had been, I'm not sure he had sufficient processing power to handle much of an explanation. Suzanne and I grabbed our carry-ons and got ready to get off the bus. "Hey!" he called out to me as we turned to go, motioning to me with his hand grasping at the air as he leaned in toward me to bequeath his sage wisdom. I turned back and he slowly added, as he pointed an unsteady finger in our direction, "Just some friendly advice for you." I waited patiently as his words wafted towards my face, soaked in the scent of alcohol. I figured it would take a bit for him to get it all out, which it did. Slowly, he continued. "Before you get home, change!" Then he added, shaking his head while half sighing, half mumbling, "I'm serious."

"Thanks for the tip." I said, smirking at him from behind my turban as I turned to escort my one-woman harem up the staircase and into the coach-class seats that awaited us.

We settled into our seats, both grateful that neither drunken businessmen nor any soused oil tycoons headed to Paris for the weekend were seated nearby. The plane's wheels retracted shortly thereafter as we began our ascent off of the dark continent. We reached cruising altitude and, as expected, began receiving our trays of food. This was an event I'd been waiting for over a month. Though we rarely used them in Chad, I readily recognized the silverware and napkin, vaguely remembering how I had once used them in what seemed to be another life, far away. And the food! Variety! Colors! Calories! Oh, and real juice! What joy! It was almost too much for me. Luckily, I was already sitting down and had my seatbelt fastened.

Well, as they say, all good things must come to an end. I had no sooner taken two bites of the freshest, greenest salad I had seen since Paris when I heard the flight attendant over the PA system make a request: If there were a doctor on board, would he please press the flight-attendant button to make himself known. I stopped chewing and thought, "I didn't really just hear that, did I? I think I did. Humph ... I didn't know my French was that good."

I wondered how it was that suddenly I could chew food and understand French at the same time. This was certainly new. Why is it that your language skills seem to just reach a usable level right when you no longer need them? And furthermore, how did they manage to time this apparent emergency with my second bite of dinner? Some days I think that part of the internship orientation should include official notice that, from then on, a doctor should never again in his life expect to have a meal without interruptions.

Like a prairie dog, I lifted my head up as I stretched my back to look around the cabin in hope that I wasn't the only guy on the plane who had graduated from medical school. Glancing around, slowly chewing what I knew, deep down, was probably the last bite of salad I was going to have for a long time, I watched for signs of any good Samaritans. None. "Guess it's just me then," I thought. I reached up and pressed the button.

The purser quickly walked back to my row and leaned over toward me. "Are you a doctor, sir?"

"Yes, I am," I said. "I just finished helping out at a hospital here in Chad for a month. What can I do for you?"

"There's a young lady up front who is not well at all. But before we proceed, can I ask if you have a copy of your license that proves you are a doctor?" I stared back at him for a moment, speechless, while in my mind I had a flashback to over a year ago. It involved an email exchange between James and me as I was planning this trip:

Me: Should I bring a copy of my medical license?

James: Dude, I taught the janitor how to do C-sections for times when I had to be away from the hospital. You're not going to need it.

I slowly emerged from the fog of my own memories; the purser was still looking at me expectantly. "You understand, I'm sure. We have to require it for legal reasons."

"No problem," I answered as I fully returned to the present time. It was understandable, I suppose. After all, at the moment, I looked more like a camel trader than an anesthesiologist. In an attempt to look more like a doctor and less like a nomad, I stepped out into the aisle and with a quick pull over my head, I shed the Arab-looking garb that I had put on over my very American-looking, military-style, gray cargo pants and black T-shirt.

Promising to show the PDFs of my credentials, which I had brought with me on a thumb drive, the purser promptly escorted me up to the bulkhead behind the cockpit, where the passenger was lying down on the floor, covered up to the neck with a blanket. I asked the purser to bring me the plane's medical kit while a stewardess, who spoke both French and English, answered my questions and acted as my interpreter. The passenger had been crying and vomiting and was deteriorating psychologically to the point where she no longer seemed to remember where she was or why she was there. Prior to reaching this point, the crew had learned that she was traveling alone to Paris to be with relatives, against her own wishes. As I listened, I knelt down beside here there in the cramped floor space, put my hand on her shoulder, and in broken French introduced myself, doing my best to explain who I was and what I was doing. From then on, I relied on the interpreter.

After I had finished taking a set of vitals and performing a brief exam, I asked a few questions through the interpreter in an effort to narrow down the possible problems this girl might be experiencing. As I listened to the answers, I looked her over to see what I could learn from simple observation, a habit I had learned early on during other trips to countries where I couldn't understand what anyone was saying. The expression on her face was a combination of fatigue, anxiety, and nausea. Yet, she was a very pretty girl, dressed in what was easily noted in Africa as being unusually new looking clothes. The jeans and sneakers were uncharacteristic for an Arab woman, though her jewelry, perfume and hand tattoos were classic for the local Arab culture. Her response to a male stranger being a little too close for comfort was classic, too, so I tried to be respectful.

During a break in the questioning, the purser leaned down towards me and in a thick French accent asked, "What we really need to know from you, Doctor, is whether or not we should turn the plane around and return her to N'Djamena for medical care, or if she is well enough to continue to Paris and be checked out there?" I thought for a few seconds. She seemed alright for now. And if that changed, would I really recommend treatment in central Africa over Western Europe? If it were me, where would I want to land in a few hours and meet an ambulance for a trip to the hospital?

Like Ronald Reagan always would, I began stating my opinion on a matter of importance by saying, "Well …" then pausing, for dramatic effect, before continuing. "Her vital signs are stable, she's appropriately responsive, for someone who's sick and been woken up for prodding and questioning at one o'clock in the morning. Having worked in the hospitals there, I see little to be gained by going back and little risk for her by flying on to Paris. As she is, I would fly on and if things change, I can reassess and let you know. For now, she's okay. We have some medicine in the kit here for nausea. Let's give her that, then see if she can drink a little so she doesn't get dehydrated."

"Fine. I'll inform the captain," he said as he turned to go. The stewardess then escorted me and the girl to first class where they had two seats open. There, we would sit side by side through the night, and I would monitor her condition for the rest of the flight.

After her dry heaves subsided, I was able to make a little conversation. I learned her name and where she had studied French. I had trouble understanding why she didn't want to go to Paris but inferred that there were cultural factors persuading her to do something that she was so adamantly opposed to that her body was literally retching.

The distinction between us was palpable. It would have been difficult to pair up two people whose backgrounds were more divergent. I had grown up with a single parent in a conservative, Protestant Christian home with few financial resources. She was from a wealthy Arabic family clan, the head of which quite likely had more than just one wife. She was being forced to leave Africa with promises of a better life. I had volunteered to come to Africa to work with no compensation, living in conditions one would normally choose to avoid. She had tight curly black hair in long, decorated braids surrounding a uniformly dark bronze complexion. In comparison, I had shorter, limp brown curls around a pale face, with newly acquired freckles, courtesy of her native Saharan sun. I thought and believed American things in English, whereas she was Arabic, educated around Muslims, and sent to French-speaking schools. And here at 38,000 feet, along with the condensation trails, our divergent lives had crisscrossed.

She never seemed to want to look me in the eye. I wondered if she resented the fact that she had an American male doctor taking care of her. I wondered if she hated me, or at least feared what she may have been told that I represented. I didn't know. There was no way I could know, for sure. Maybe I didn't need to.

Other than one more set of dry heaves, she did fine the rest of the way to Paris, and both of us got some needed sleep. When we landed, she was the first passenger off. Someone met her with a wheelchair, and I watched her slowly walk out of the cabin with the stewardess at her side. I wondered what would happen to her. Stretching my legs as I stood, I tried to awaken myself more fully. I went back to coach to collect my carry-on, meet Suzanne, and then exit with everyone else. As we stepped off the plane and turned to walk up the gently sloping ramp to the concourse I nearly ran into the girl, who was seated in her wheelchair; airline representatives were about to transport her and her luggage to the waiting ambulance parked on the tarmac below. I stopped. She looked up, a weary look on her face. I smiled, addressed her by name and said, "Salaam aleikum." Her face immediately lit up, and with a very big smile she replied, "Aleikum asalaam." Then I turned and walked away, knowing that my best had been good enough.

The six-hour layover in Paris was longer than I liked. Suzanne and I stretched out on the seats near our terminal, set the clock alarm, and tried to get some more sleep without the fitful fear of missing our flights. I was headed to Atlanta, where I would change planes yet again before traveling on to Omaha. Her flight was nonstop to San Francisco. After a bit of a nap, each of us did our best to snap out of the dreamlike state that seems to slowly fade as you travel "home" after being in a radically different place. We consoled ourselves by reviewing a couple of pictures we'd taken during the trip, and made promises to burn and exchange CDs to complete each other's collection of photos. Eventually, though, we had to say goodbye, and after one last hug and a wave, she boarded her plane and I walked back to my own terminal from where I departed shortly thereafter.

I don't remember much of that flight. But I will say that it always seems to me that when your plane lands in America, the touchdown is always a relief, if not always smooth. Another thing that struck me was that no one cheered. It used to be that whenever a flight from a foreign country touched down on U.S. soil every American on the plane would cheer and burst into applause. That never seems to happen anymore. At least, not on Air France.

I nonchalantly made my way off the plane and made a quick stop at the very first bathroom to pull off my Arabian version of overalls before reaching the customs and immigration checkpoint. Like superman, I promptly emerged from my blink-of-an-eye transformation and strode towards passport control like I owned the place, my clothes, turban, and silver rimmed Ray-Bans deftly and innocently concealed within my backpack.

As I stood in line to get accepted back into the Motherland, I got out the letters of invitation to Chad, anticipating the questions I would have to answer regarding why I had gone. My turn came, and the officer motioned for me to come forward. I handed him my passport as I greeted him. He calmly took my passport and landing card without responding. He looked them over for a bit and then after a quick, perfunctory stamp, returned my passport and simply said, "Welcome home, son."

"Thanks," I said. At least that's what I think I said out loud because on the inside I was blathering in an obsequious tone saying, "I … I … I love you, man!" Stifling my inner voice from declaring itself in what might have been an embarrassing public outburst of patriotism, I retained my outward composure and went merrily on my way to collect my bags before flying the final leg of my journey to Omaha, Nebraska.

There are mixed sensations for anyone returning from one of these kinds of life-altering trips. There's both good and bad mixed together. You're glad and yet, at the same time, sad. It's like feeling the warm sun shine on your face during a bitter, cold and cloudless winter day. There's certainly a great sense of accomplishment that accompanies any challenging endeavor of this nature. But I find it diluted to some degree by regret, stemming from the knowledge that so much remains undone. I have learned to cope with this latter, negative portion of my feelings by firmly accepting the fact that my mission is not to be the Savior of the world. I simply represent Him. Doing so does not make it my personal responsibility to right all the wrongs, fix all the problems, or even soothe all the wounds. I can only do what is humanly possible. That which I can do, that which I promise to others and to myself is to make an effort when and where I can to the best of my abilities. Then, I move on, having succeeded in taking actions that produced unique results. Results that occurred only because I was there. Do I fail at times? Sure. But I don't fail to try.

If and when there are people who can continue working despite your absence, that's great. You stretch your final efforts as you pass the baton, letting them run their leg of the race, unhindered by the fetters of your own regrets or disappointments. What's hard, though, is leaving a place without anyone remaining to do what you were doing. For medical providers, it is then that you are most vulnerable to haunting thoughts of suffering, death, and dying, which you imagine yourself being able to prevent, if only you were there. The self-inflicted guilt that is an outgrowth of these illusions is very real, though I believe, unnecessary.

The taxi cab pulled into my driveway. I climbed out into the cold night air, almost 100 degrees cooler than the highs I had become accustomed to in Chad. My breath frosted the air and formed miniature clouds over my numb fingers as I fumbled with the keys, trying to unlock the front door of my house. Moments later, standing on the inside, shutting the door against the cold outside, I sighed heavily as I stood silently in the dark foyer of a place I called home. Finally, I had arrived. And I knew it.

I had arrived, not at a place but at a point in life. A point where I was really living a life that was right for me. It was a destination that subconsciously I had been seeking all along, although the quest had triggered previously unconscious fears of getting lost forever or never even finding my way, like Ponce de Leon seeking his fountain of youth. Yet I'd had the good fortune of catching a glimpse of this magical destination that most never reach, let alone believe in. People seem to sadly wander through life, merely getting old and dying before they find their own personal path on which to walk, having lived their entire life following someone else's road map. The purchase price for the ticket that brought me to this point was paid by giving up my illusions of financial security, personal security, and the social acceptance obtained by pursuing everyone else's idea of the American dream. I chose instead to do what I did simply because *it was what I wanted* for myself out of life. I did what I wanted, with whom I wanted, for as long as I wanted. And as it turned out, exercising this level of personal freedom was intoxicating. But it took a great amount of willpower to take action. It took the will to do only what I believed would make me happy and bring a sense of fulfillment just because I tried. I also had to calmly, respectfully, cover my ears with both hands to block out the dissonant chorus of authoritative voices telling me what I should want, what I should do, what should make me happy and content. I can't even hear them anymore.

It was through that silence that I dragged my two suitcases up the stairs, past the still-barren refrigerator door, down the short hallway and back to the master bedroom, wearily leaning the bags against the foot of the bed. Nearly fifty-two hours after I awoke from my Chadian sleep on a uncomfortably thin foam pad and pushed aside the mosquito net to turn off the sound of its alarm, I lifted my travel-size, short-wave clock radio out of my shoulder bag and put it back in its proper place on the corner of the nightstand. Then, I smiled to myself as I turned the alarm off and slowly slid into my own bed. But not before taking three very hot, very soapy showers in a row.

Postscript

Shortly after arriving back in the states, I got word from James regarding the little boy we had taken care of during our last case. His family had taken him home, having essentially lost hope. And it was there that he had died. Despite the disappointment, I consoled myself with the fact that we had done all we could, for as long as we could, the best we knew how. I suppose it could have been worse. Sometimes I just don't know. But I have come to the point where I no longer feel as though I have to know. It's like one of my professors in medical school taught me. You don't have to know everything to know enough.

About the Author

Former Assistant Professor of Anesthesiology at the University of Nebraska, Dr. Cobos resigned from his position and left his pursuits in research and scholarly publications in order to teach and provide anesthesia as a volunteer in developing countries. He has delivered babies in Papua New Guinea, held the heads of the dying in Kenya, laughed while trying to speak Chichewa in Malawi, and in this volume describes his medical mission in the Republic of Chad, Africa. He owns a house in Omaha, Nebraska, and even stays there on occasion when he's in the United States. For all inquiries, including appearances, book signing events, and upcoming releases, contact the author at ItCouldBeWorseCobos@gmail.com.

Appendix: Advice for Newbies

With the benefit of hindsight, I present the top ten things you need to know about living in the mission field, should you ever choose to go. This list is by no means exhaustive, though I might say it was certainly exasperating to develop. It is based upon the wisdom gained through personal experience and the misguided use of bad judgment during the first half of my trip to Chad. It is presented with hopes that you will gain valuable insight, after having a good laugh.

Friendly mission tip #1: When packing important things to bring along, consider the Navy SEAL's slogan, "Two is one, and one is none."

Friendly mission tip #2: While in the WC, consider the water conservationist's motto, "If it's yellow, let it mellow. If it's brown, flush it down."

Friendly mission tip #3: As you shop at the market, recall that your thickly accented conversation starting with "How much does the … cost?" is quickly and universally interpreted to mean, "I want to barter. I have much money to spend. I have no idea how much I should be paying for what you are selling me. Make a very high opening bid, then enjoy yourself at my own expense, while you make a killing haggling over the price with me."

Friendly mission tip #4: When visiting the locals, do not insult them by turning down their offer to drink some tea. Even though it may be 98 degrees in the shade where you're sitting together, and the tea is actually steaming.

Friendly mission tip #5: It's okay to shake hands with everybody, even though you don't know them, don't know what's been on their hands, don't know if they even know how to wash their hands, or if they pick their rotten teeth or their nose with more than one finger while they shake hands with you. Just wash your own hands before touching your face. And, if there's sufficient water that night at the house, take three showers.

Friendly mission tip #6: If you can actually see a stinger on the wasp as it flies by, do not, I repeat, do not take a swing at it with your bare hand. Use the fly swatter. It's probably next to the stove.

Friendly mission tip #7: When you feel something crawling in your pants, do not smash it directly against your skin. Instead, grip it between two bunched up layers of clothing using your fingers, then smash it to death, letting its crunchy remnants fall harmlessly out your pant leg as you walk away as if nothing at all out of the ordinary has just transpired.

Friendly mission tip #8: Remember, each time you use toilet paper to blow your nose brings you that many little paper squares closer to having to use your left hand later on, in the end (so to speak).

Friendly mission tip #9: Hear me now and believe me later on, but when the soldier holding the Kalashnikov in his lap and riding in the back of the only functioning automobile within a fifty-mile radius shakes his finger in the universally understood "No, no" motion as you raise your digital camera in his general direction, do not take his picture (while he's still looking at you).

Friendly mission tip #10: Before cracking any eggs, check to see if they float. An egg that sinks will likely taste good. If it floats, keep it in a secure location, preferably under lock and key, ready to be launched by hand, sling, or trebuchet, if and when civil war breaks out. I assure you, you will be on the winning side, if you're upwind.

Made in the USA
San Bernardino, CA
14 January 2014